THESE MY PEOPLE

Jeannie Montgomery

authorHOUSE®

AuthorHouse™
1663 Liberty Drive, Suite 200
Bloomington, IN 47403
www.authorhouse.com
Phone: 1-800-839-8640

© *2008 Jeannie Montgomery. All rights reserved.*

No part of this book may be reproduced, stored in a retrieval system, or transmitted by any means without the written permission of the author.

First published by AuthorHouse 2/13/2008

ISBN: 978-1-4343-6187-5 (sc)

Library of Congress Control Number: 2008901204

Printed in the United States of America
Bloomington, Indiana

This book is printed on acid-free paper.

ACKNOWLEDGEMENTS

My special thanks to my sister Cecile Brunson who spent hours correcting my English.

My deep gratitude to my friends who encouraged me to keep writing.

My thanks to my husband who helped proof-read and edit this book.

DEDICATION

This book is dedicated:

To my loving husband because he shared with me every mile, every trial, every smile and every victory.

To my dear children because they were with us through everything we did.

To my grandchildren so they can know the grandparents they grew up without.

Contents

ACKNOWLEDGEMENTS v
DEDICATION vii
INTRODUCTION xi

CHAPTER ONE 1
Growing up in Central Louisiana

CHAPTER TWO 25
Off to Japan

CHAPTER THREE 31
Japan 1954-1957

CHAPTER FOUR 45
Getting Priorities Straight 1957

CHAPTER FIVE 49
Getting Started in Brazil 1958-1960

CHAPTER SIX 66
Frontier Life in Pioneiros 1960-1961

CHAPTER SEVEN 88
Pereira Barreto 1961-1963

CHAPTER EIGHT 94
Back to Jabaquara The Revolution of 1964

CHAPTER NINE 110
Santa Cruz Do Rio Pardo A New Door Opens 1965-1977

CHAPTER TEN 149
Pereira Barreto 1977-1990

CHAPTER ELEVEN 170
Special Problems In Sud Menucci 1977-1989

CHAPTER TWELVE 175
Ourinhos 1989-2001

INTRODUCTION

"What in the world am I doing here so far from Grant Parish?" I asked myself once, when the sudden strangeness of the place where we were addled me.

Of course I knew the answer, but my senses were dulled from breathing in the red dust stirred up by the truck in front of us. When the vehicle carried its dust storm on down the road and the red cloud settled down, I could see clearly the reason why we were here. All along the road, new lands were partially cleared, and little shacks had been thrown up in a hurry. Men were clearing away the underbrush and chopping down young trees in a race against time to make a crop to feed their families. Others were digging the ground with nothing more than a hoe. Some places already had little tender shoots of corn or some vegetables coming up among the stumps to ensure a fast crop for their immediate needs. The women worked side by side with their men. There had been no time to dig a well. Amidst this scenery I saw a woman carrying a five-gallon bucket of water balanced on her head as she climbed the steep hill. That in itself was no big feat for a pioneer woman, but she also carried another bucket just like it in one hand while she swung a crutch under the other arm. She had only one leg with which to climb. How well that woman adapted to her situation without any modern device! I marveled, and at the same time, I knew why we had moved out here to the "Far West" of Brazil. In 1960 nearly all these country people had never seen a Bible, and many could not even read. Very few had heard of the Gospel in this area away from the big cities. That is why we were here. Like the one legged woman, I knew I must adapt.

I don't know just when the change came that I no longer thought of myself as being in a strange land. It was a gradual thing with me, as Brazil became my home and its people became my people. The strangeness disappeared as the landmarks took on that common everyday look of home because home was just around the corner.

As I slowly became integrated into another culture, my own native land and childhood seemed very distant. It was more like something I had dreamed and not what I had lived. Yet I owed my very being and even the reason as to why I was on the mission field to my roots here in Central Louisiana.

Missionary work has been the heartbeat of my home church as long as I can remember. We not only were taught to give liberally to missions but we also had a constant flow of missionaries to come and speak for us. Our prayers always mentioned the missionaries on the foreign fields. My love for missions was no greater than that of the other members of Corinth Baptist Church. Now when I see the faithfulness of some of the peers of my youth, I wonder why the Lord didn't choose one more worthy than myself to go on the mission field. For whatever reason the Lord might have had, I am not sorry that I went; I only wish I had another life to give. It is good, though, to have had people who loved the Lord support us with prayers the forty-seven years we were on the foreign mission field. For this I will be eternally grateful.

"Not named" Garlington was the name that appeared on my birth certificate. Later Aunt Maggie, my old maid aunt who lived with us, made an affidavit stating that my name was Eugenia. I have often wondered exactly what kind of expectations my parents, Oliver and Alice Garlington, had for me, if any at all. Perhaps they wanted me to be a boy and didn't bother to pick out a girl's name, or maybe they were so tired of having children until the prospect of having a seventh child had left them lethargic. They had used up a long list of names already on my older siblings: Nathan Auzell, Esther Mae, Timothy O'Donald, Margaret Alice, Cecile Frances, and Leonard Oliver. Four years after my birth I guess they had recuperated enough to have a name waiting for my baby sister, Mary Beth. However my real name was only recorded when I had to get my marriage certificate for a passport to travel abroad. Everyone called me Jeannie but I assumed that they wanted my real name to be Eugenia like that of an old maid schoolteacher, Eugenia Garrett. Perhaps my family hoped that one day I would follow in her footsteps. They missed out on both counts; I was neither an old maid nor a schoolteacher. I married a missionary.

When Steve Montgomery came into my life, I was not looking for a husband. In fact, I had determined in my heart to remain single unless I knew it was God's will for me to marry. It was as much a surprise to me as to anyone that God sent him my way. Since the day that we married, December 20, 1953, I have never doubted that our marriage was God's will for us. Based on God's will, our love has endured the test of time. It was because of a mutual love for God and each other that our world has stretched from Dry Prong, Louisiana, across our continent to embrace the peoples of the far corners of the earth: from Japan to Brazil and even Africa.

Since I had married a stranger, I had a lot to learn about him and he about me. Before Steve was born, his parents, Hallie and Audie Montgomery, made God a promise that if He would give them a son, their fifth child would be given back to Him. They had lost an infant son before Steve was born, and they wanted God to have this one for

His service. Wisely, his parents did not tell him what they had prayed until he was grown and had begun to preach. In this way, they would be sure God was doing the calling and not themselves. It was no surprise to them when Steve announced that the Lord was calling him to preach and then later to be a missionary. Always giving their blessings, they never once objected to his going to foreign lands even when they knew they would never see him again here on earth. He has also had the moral support of his brothers Truitt and Ray, and his sisters, Jean, Sue, Lou, and Shirley.

Our union opened up a whole new life for me. He was on his way to Japan as a missionary, and I was in nurse's training when we married. When my obligations ended in February of 1954, we said good-bye to our families and friends and immediately headed for Chicago to get my entrance visa to go to Japan as his wife. Also he wanted me to meet the Antioch Missionary Baptist Church of Greencastle, Indiana, who had set Steve apart as a missionary. We then visited several more churches at their requests as we headed for Japan.

Although God had already taught me to rely heavily on Him in my youth, this was a total immersion into a walk by faith. I wish I could say that my faith was so strong I never was afraid of anything, but the truth of the matter is that I was and still am nothing more than a scaredy-cat, dependent on God to do what I cannot do myself.

On the West Coast we joined another couple and set sail for Japan May 1, 1954, arriving seventeen days later. We worked there for nearly three years before returning to the States and then leaving for Brazil.

Japan was where we first learned of the tremendous flow of Japanese immigrants to Brazil. After we had a good working knowledge of the language and helped to start a church in Tokyo, we had numerous encounters with people going to São Paulo, Brazil. Many started asking us why didn't we go to Brazil; thus the seed was planted in our hearts to go there as missionaries. After many direct answers to prayer in making our final decision to go, we sailed back to Seattle on the same ship on which we had gone to Japan. This time we brought back with us two little Montgomerys, Jonathan David and Donald Timothy. Deborah Jean joined us in Louisiana on the way to Brazil. The rest of our children, Michael Ray, Rebekah Ann, and Steven Eugene would make their appearances later in Brazil.

Not everyone understood our change of fields; some even ridiculed. Looking back now over all these years, we know without a shadow of a doubt, we did the right thing. God did indeed lead us to work in Brazil. Although we left some people dear to our hearts in Japan, our lives were chiefly devoted to a people on the very opposite side of the earth. The major part of this book will be devoted to telling about our Brazilian people although I want to give a brief picture of all of my people.

I have been requested by many friends here and in Brazil to give to them a written history of our life and work. Certainly, each one has a right to know since without them I would have no story to tell and this book would not be possible.

History and truth are not always "politically correct." I apologize to any who prefers not to be remembered in connection with us or with any circumstances written in this book. In relating any situation given here, I do not wish to offend in any way the people mentioned. But, if in this book you can hear me singing with Jeremiah, "Great is thy faithfulness," then I will have accomplished my purpose. I only want my readers to see what God has done for all of us, and what He can do for all who trust Him.

My family, my church community, my Japanese brethren, and my Brazilian spiritual family, all *These, My People,* are my priceless heritage. I want you to meet them and know a little about them and their lands.

CHAPTER ONE
Growing up in Central Louisiana

It all started many years ago right here in Central Louisiana in the little rural community of my home church, the Corinth Baptist Church. Our community was so unpretentious until the only time one of our names made the "Daily Town Talk" was when it appeared in the obituary column. I was born among the people who populated this area. Many were related to me, either paternally or maternally. If perchance they weren't, our families were so close, the children called the older ones uncle and aunt anyway. At church we were just one big family. That was the way it was when I was growing up between the 1930's and 1950's in Grant Parish.

Flagon Creek flowed between the lands belonging to my dad's people, the Garlingtons, on the east and my mother's, the Tisons, on the west. There were plenty of wooded lands between them where we children roamed like open range cattle. This was the "boot camp" for my life's work.

To an outsider we were nothing more than a bunch of poor hillbillies the modern world had bypassed. The plain, unpainted look of our dwellings belied the fact that we were in truth a community greatly blessed. When I was young, a northern lady once said to me that our houses down South looked like their barns up North. For the first time in my life I was embarrassed about where I lived and how I was brought up. She made me see our lives through the eyes of an outsider. I didn't like what I saw. Rusty tin roofs on old weather beaten houses spoke volumes about our financial status. The barns, the smoke houses, the cowsheds, and even the toilets matched the dilapidated look of our houses. The open wells told the world that we didn't have running water and maybe no electricity. It all blinded me from seeing what we really had. The extent of my travels had been confined within Grant Parish with the exception of those times Daddy took me to Alexandria to pick out a new pair of shoes. My knowledge of other places was nil and I could not see, what I now know to be true, that we lived in a child's paradise. This place was teeming with innocent and healthy things for children to do. Every tree was there to be climbed and every creek was there for some child to watch crawfish shoot out of sight if disturbed. Our imaginations could take wings when we looked for ancient Indian burial grounds beneath some mound near the sands where we dug for arrowheads along the banks of Flagon. Violets, dogwoods, and honeysuckles were all over the place in spring. It was very gratifying indeed to be nature's children in this unrecognized place, but nature was not the chief character forming influence of the Corinth community. That distinction belonged to the Bible loving people who populated this area.

Since the Garlingtons lived on the eastside of Flagon and the Tisons on the westside, it was almost inevitable that sooner or later some of the offspring of both parties would marry. It happened with my mother and daddy. I don't know who first moved here, but I think it was Mother's people, the Tisons.

THE TISONS

My maternal ancestors known by the name of Tison or Tyson were some of the original settlers of the town of Dry Prong. The colorful history of the Tisons goes back to the beginning of the settlement of Houston, Texas, where some of our ancestors, the Vinces, owned huge tracts of property and at one time furnished cattle to feed Sam Houston's army. A couple of generations later my great, great Grandfather William settled here. His prolific bunch bought lands along Highway 167 from the present town of Dry Prong to within a few miles of the Rapides Parish's border where Grandpa Job Tison and his children settled in what is now our community. He fathered 12 children by my Grandmother Frances who already had one son by her first husband.

Unfortunately, I never knew my grandmother Frances Richardson Tison; but judging by her six daughters, she must have been a gentle soul. She was a charter member of one of the older Baptist Churches of Alexandria before moving out here. Without a doubt she taught her children well. These girls became the spiritual backbone of our community.

On the other hand, Grandpa Job lived to become the family legend.

GRANDPA JOB

Standing on grounds, which once bore my father's name, I sensed that something as simple as raking leaves had triggered a stir of my ancestral genes even though it had been nearly half a century since I had lived in these parts. I had no trouble identifying whose they were. The urge to strike a match and let the fire do the work for me told me exactly whose genes were trying to dominate. Grandpa Job Tison, my mama's papa, loved a good fire. He enjoyed building a fire so big its tongues would often reach beyond the confines of the fireplace as if to lick away the pain of his "ole achy bones." Lying on a pallet in front of the hearth, he was at peace with the world. Nevertheless the gentle daughters of Job stood by constantly on guard with buckets of water handy to douse the flames in case he set something on fire. His affinity with fire got him into trouble more than once and if I were not careful, the present pastor of Corinth Baptist Church would have a hard time explaining to his congregation why his wife had burned off the whole parsonage lot.

Before you draw some wrong conclusion about my most interesting Grandpa, let me explain. He was a stickler for his legal rights. This fairly well educated man was not a lawyer like his famous cousin Huey P. Long, but he should have been. I remember seeing his old thick law books stacked in our quilt closet waiting for him to use their contents to confuse the judge or law officers. That was where the danger lay. For example, he had found some unknown "right" to stake a claim on government land and persistently tried to do so in the middle of the Kisatche National Forest, where my Dad worked hard to preserve this disappearing treasure. Since Grandpa had been a widower before I was born, he lived here and there among his children but preferred to stay out in a little shanty on "his claim." Those were the times when the strong urge would hit him to burn off his claim and show his rightful ownership. As far as my Dad was concerned that was an official and personal declaration of war with him because he would have to go out with a crew to fight Grandpa's fire. After the fire was quenched, it was then Dad's duty to haul Grandpa into court. During such occasions things were pretty stressful for the gentle daughters of Job around our house, but after awhile things would calm down with everyone dismissing the episode by saying that Grandpa had been a little touched in the head ever since he had had a sun stroke when he was fifty. Of course, the law was not so tolerant with him when he was called to appear in court on several occasions. He always refused to accept the help of lawyers because he thought he knew more than they and could argue his own cause. Big mistake! He never won a case until a little before he died when the judge finally admitted that Grandpa was right. The matter was dropped when no one pursued the case after his demise.

One of the first poems I learned in my childhood came about because of Grandpa's regular appearances before the court. The judge, tired of hearing Grandpa's arguments reprimanded him once by reciting this old rhyme:

There was an old owl who sat in the oak.

The more he heard, the less he spoke.

The less he spoke, the more he heard.

It would be wise for you to imitate that ole bird.

Because, for some reason or other, the gentle daughters of Job thought it necessary to quote that poem to me frequently; I remember it until this day. Its author was unknown as was the case with many of the old ballads and poems, which especially Aunt Maggie who lived with us could quote exactly on the right occasion to teach us kids a lesson we needed to learn.

Grandpa carried his obsession with the law over into his religious beliefs. He was not a member of our church but was more like a Seventh Day Baptist than anything else. He devotedly observed the Sabbath on Saturday as the Law of Moses demanded. He also was not addicted to drinking or smoking; in short, he was a good man in spite of being argumentative.

One thing that he excelled in was getting his point over. Back before the dangers of tobacco were known, he and the grandfather of my brother-in-law, Murwyn Welch, argued whether or not a Christian should smoke. Grandpa Job said, "Not at all."

Grandpa Welch argued the opposite. To prove that no spiritual harm could be done by smoking, he quoted Matthew 15:11: "Not that which goeth into the mouth defileth a man; but that which cometh out of the mouth, this defileth a man."

"Then why in this world don't you swallow the stuff?" was Grandpa Job's quelling rebuttal.

It was because of his blind spot about the law, that Mama and Aunt Maggie doubted if he really understood salvation by grace through faith. and not by our works. Works are the result, not the cause of our salvation. I guess he got that all straightened out before he died because when he was about to breath his last, he looked up to heaven and said, "I see angels coming for me." This was a tremendous comfort to his children, and we all hoped that these celestial beings carried Grandpa Job straight to Abraham's Bosom.

The day he was buried it rained so hard no one except those needed to put him to rest, were able to go to the cemetery after the brief funeral services at our house. Apparently there must have been some hush-hush talk among the adults as to where his soul might have gone when he died because we small children had our own wild theory. "He must have gone to heaven since, don't you know, if it rains when a person dies, that's a sure sign he went to heaven?"

Grandpa Job, who was born during the Civil War and died during the first part of World War II, lies near many of his children in the Frazier Cemetery a few miles from here, but when I drive around these parts and see some cousin of mine out burning off the grounds, I smile because I know Grandpa's genes are still alive and doing very well, thank you.

There is a story behind every one of his children but other than that of my mother, Aunt Maggie's life is the one that affected me most.

AUNT MAGGIE

Margaret Castletine Tison, better known to everybody as Aunt Maggie, came to live with my parents before I was born. When she was young, her fiancé died three months before they were to be married. Heartbroken, Aunt Maggie never married but instead became the community's live-in nanny. Her influence on all the community cannot be underestimated. She never birthed a child of her own, but was present at the birth of nearly every child around here.

I'm glad she made our house her home because that way I had two mothers. She was always the strong one physically, and we children could not fool her with our tricks. Her authority over us was not to be questioned. I can remember many times hearing Mama say, "Maggie, go spank that kid." Immediately, Aunt Maggie would tell me to go to the switch tree (a pomegranate bush which had thin limber stems) to get a switch. That was worse than the switching because I had to pick out my own instrument of punishment. It had to be just the right size, not too long, and by all means not too short. She never was harsh with her punishment, and we always knew why we were being punished. The switch never did any physical or physiological harm; in fact, it helped make decent kids out of us.

Aunt Maggie knew the Bible better than most preachers. She was a master story teller. When evening would fall, we would gather around her out on the porch or on the steps where we could see the stars above as she recited story after story. Somehow she imparted to us the knowledge of a faithful God up there who was in control, and we could trust Him completely as we listened to her make Bible stories come to life. Nearly all of her stories had a moral lesson for us to learn. For example, she put the fear of God in us about making fun of people with the story of Elisha sending out the two female bears to punish the forty-two children who had made fun of him and his bald head when he returned from performing a great miracle. To this day, I don't like to hear people make fun of someone else and I especially hate ethnic jokes.

Besides knowing the Bible from cover to cover, she knew many old folk songs which my family now laments that we did not record. There was a song for every lesson to be taught us children. If we needed admonishing because of laziness, there was one for that. The one that I remember the most teaches young people not to kill wild life just for sport. It was so touching, we would almost cry when she sang it. I think it goes something like this:

There came to my window one morning in spring,
A sweet little robin he came there to sing.
The song that he sang was sweeter by far
Than ever was played on a flute or guitar.

How happy, how happy this world seemed to be.
Awake little girl and be happy with me.
But soon as he finished his beautiful song,
A thoughtless young man with a gun came along.

He killed, and he carried my poor bird away.
No more can he sing at the break of the day.

Her balance between tenderness and toughness was amazing. While she never shot at anything for sport, she knew how to load up our double barrel gun and run off any "varmint" if it posed a threat.

These My People

When chewing gum first came out on the market, Aunt Maggie was in grammar school. The teacher would buy gum and chew it first. Then the student who made the highest grade in spelling had the prize of chewing it next. Aunt Maggie was a perfect speller, so she always had the privilege of chewing her teacher's second hand gum while it still had a little of its original flavor. This sounds awful to us today, but let us remember that chewing gum was a novelty back then. The only gum those children had ever chewed was rosin collected from the plentiful sweet gum trees in this area. (By the way, sweet gum rosin has a very pleasant taste; I use to chew it myself.)

Aunt Maggie was an amazing woman. With her ability to innovate, she saved Mary Beth's life at birth. Mary was born prematurely without the nursing instinct. All of the babies were born at home back then, so a person had to take things in hand and do what could be done or wait for death. Aunt Maggie wasn't one to sit idly by. Besides keeping the baby warm, she also took a piece of bacon rind and pulled it in and out of Mary's mouth until she developed the sucking reflex. Gradually Mary improved and soon became a healthy little girl thanks to Aunt Maggie.

She was a "Jack of all trades." Her versatility, whether teaching us kids history, cooking, sewing, farming, or how to adapt to a difficult situation, without a doubt made her the perfect tutor for a future missionary's wife.

While Aunt Maggie was the physically and intellectually strong one around our house, Mama was considered the spiritual leader of the bunch.

MOTHER

It is hard for me to remember Mama as a well person. What I remember most before she became ill was how she was esteemed for her righteous life. When she died, I remember one of Mama's sisters-in-law, who was not of our faith, saying, "If anyone ever went to heaven, Alice did."

Once I overheard Mama sharing her faith with a lady at church concerning us kids. She quoted Psalm 37:4, "Delight thyself also in the Lord; and he shall give thee the desires of thy heart." Then she added, "My desire is that all of my children trust in the Lord and be saved."

As far as I know, God heard her request.

When I was thirteen, Mama's health rapidly declined and she never recovered. God gave me the responsibility and privilege of caring for her until her death. The hard learned lessons at that time have tempered my outlook on life ever since.

COUSINS BY THE DOZENS

Since Mama had several brothers and sisters living nearby, we all had cousins near our own age. There was a natural pairing off of kids as buddies. Mine was Nelda Honeycutt, one of Aunt Audie's daughters.

There was absolutely no need for a telephone in our community. Our own "grapevine telephone" worked beautifully. I doubt if there was anything going on around us for miles that Nelda and I didn't know and help to spread. When any little juicy tidbit of gossip reached our ears, we ran straight to our pasture fence where we could hang over it and impart the hot news to eager ears. Since most of our sisters and brothers were older, we always had an abundant supply of gossip to report about their courting episodes. As for ourselves, when we began to grow up and go our separate ways, we lost something precious. I remember crying the first time I realized that we were growing up. Our "grapevine" closeness was slowly dissipating, and its lost hurt.

Most of my daily contacts were with the Tison side of the family but we did have some good times with my Garlington kin.

THE GARLINGTONS

One of the first lessons a person should learn is: don't shake your ancestral tree too hard. You may get hit on the head by rotten fruit.

If you ever hear of the name, Garlington, it most surely belongs to some relative of mine. It is not a common name. When only one person on our family tree turns out to be a little tainted, however remote the connection may be, somehow all of us are contaminated for wearing that name. Really we do have a lot of decent folk among the Garlington ancestry, including one my grandmothers of the 18th century, who shared a grandmother with a cousin named George Washington. In fact, until I went to Texas, I was always ready to spout off about the accomplishments of my family anywhere. Most of my paternal relatives were in one fashion or another educators or military; those who weren't supported those who were. My beloved Uncle Beuron, who had a distinguished war record as a glider pilot during the invasion of Normandy, was the high school principal at Dry Prong when I graduated. The gymnasium was named for him. Others of the family have made a name for themselves also, so I was not expecting to have my family pride deflated.

Trying to make small talk with a person in East Texas one day I stated, "My maiden name is Garlington."

Jeannie Montgomery

"Garlington!" the dear little lady exclaimed. "My neighbor down the road is a Garlington. He ain't nothing but an ornery ole cuss." Then she proceeded to tell me all of his evils.

I felt like I somehow had suddenly inherited an excess of "sin" genes that normal human beings don't have. I wanted to quietly dismiss myself long enough to check out all my rotten spots to see how badly I was affected. I knew that I was a sinner saved by grace; and if it weren't for God's grace, I would be as bad off as my Texas kin. Even though I didn't know this distant relative existed before now, I wanted to go crawl under my infamous cousin's fence with all it's dangling "no trespassing signs," dodge his bullets, and embrace him so I could say, "Hey, Buddy, if God can save me, He can save you, too. God's grace can do that, you know."

Once my brother had a similar experience, probably concerning the same person, when a visiting preacher came to speak at his church. The minister could not deliver his message until he had thoroughly enlightened the congregation on how terrible this Garlington fellow in Texas was. I don't doubt that my relative was bullheaded because that trait pops up frequently among us; but this Texas relative of mine must have really been something for the books.

Now, that I have duly recorded the above incidents, I want to tell a little about the mainstream Garlington connections. As early as 1100 AD, my family has a documented history in England where my ancestors were noblemen. Our American lineage started with a Christopher Garlington who came to America in the early 17th century. There were five consecutive generations of Christophers. When Christopher III came along, he was contemporary with George Washington and fought in the armies of Cousin George for our independence. Ever since then, there have been Garlingtons in every war this country has fought. But there were many who pursued other professions. Sprinkled throughout the generations were a large number of pastors of either Methodist or Baptist persuasions. There have also been doctors and many teachers in our lineage; nevertheless, I know that there have been those who have not lived as they should.

Unlike mother's people who were predominately Baptist, my Garlington grandparents, Hensley and Mary Frances were devout Methodists. As a result of not going to church with them, I didn't feel the spiritual bond that I had with some of my Tison relatives; but I do have very fond memories of them which I would like to share with you.

GRANDPA AND GRANDMA GARLINGTON

When one of my Garlington cousins was recently buried in a plot near my grandparents in the old Springhill Cemetery, I felt a strange feeling of coming home. As my eyes caressed the familiar names chiseled out on the marble stone around me, my mind drifted from what the preacher was saying to when I was a child. I could almost feel the curved handle of Grandpa's walking cane reach out around my neck and draw me into his lap as he did every time Dad took us little ones to visit them on Saturdays. Although I never once heard him say, "I love you," I knew he did; his walking cane told me that. He was already an old man when I was born. He and Grandma tried their best to please us young ones. I can't remember anything outstanding about him other than that he had a sharp mind until he died at the ripe old age of 95.

Grandma was another story. Beneath her thin ball of reddish white hair was a woman of strength and tenderness much like the early pioneer women of our country. If I were to draw her picture, I would have to put a big bowl of peaches and cream in one hand and a broomstick in the other.

At home Mother never let me drink coffee unless it was when I took castor oil or quinine to get the taste out of my mouth. (Those were the two medicines that cured everything in those days before penicillin came along!) But at Grandma's house, it was different. I was whisked out of my dad's sight soon after arrival and treated to a cup of delicious coffee so full of cream you could almost make butter out of it, or in fruit season I would be treated to her wonderful peaches. Grandma gave me what she liked best; and that is why I didn't have to learn to like *"café com leite"* (coffee with milk*)* when I went to Brazil; I was back in Grandma's kitchen.

Grandma was a brave and strong soul. The story goes that once when all the men folk were away, a robber entered her house. Since only she and her daughter were there, without hesitating she grabbed up her broom and literally drove the offender away single handedly with only a broom. What a woman!

When she and Grandpa celebrated their 69th wedding anniversary, I was still in high school but thought I was big enough to handle anything. I decided to bake them a big wedding cake, which looked more like the leaning tower of Pisa than a wedding cake. Its only redeeming quality was that there was plenty to go around. Grandma loved it anyway.

I was already on my way to the mission field when Grandma died, but I hardly ever drink a cup of coffee with milk or eat a big juicy white peach without thinking of her. I loved my Grandma!

Grandma and Grandpa Garlington had ten children, seven boys and three girls. One of the girls died as a teenager. The older brothers did not have the opportunity to study more than the seventh grade, but they had such a hunger for education, they helped pay for their younger siblings to go to college. That was one of the most outstanding things about my daddy.

DADDY

Daddy was well known around here. So much so until one day when one of Mama's elderly aunts came to visit us by bus, she told the driver to stop at Oliver Garlington's house. Being from another town, he didn't know Daddy.

Exasperated, Aunt Rose shouted at him, "You don't know Oliver Garlington? Why, everybody knows Oliver!"

The driver might not have known Daddy, but she was nearly right. In the depression Daddy was a foreman with the WPA and later the CCC. During World War II he was foreman of the maintenance crew at the Pollock Air Base. After the War he was foreman of the work force of the government owned Stuart Nursery which ensured a continual supply of pine seedlings for reforestation in Kisatche National Forest. An untold number of people worked with him from all the areas around here during his lifetime.

Since he was so well known, he was either loved or hated. Nearly all the young people, especially my sister's boyfriends, were extremely fearful of him.

He did have a soft spot though. Once I heard him say, "If you educate a man, you have educated only one person; but if you educate a woman, you have educated a family." That was why he tried to educate all five of his daughters.

One other thing I like to remember about Daddy was his generosity. He had a unique way of teaching us children to give to the church. Instead of giving the offering out of his pocket himself, he divided what he wanted to give among us children and let us give it. He gave, but at the same time, we also learned to give.

The characteristic which stands out most about him was his independent, self relying attitude. He was that way until the day he died. For fear that he would leave one little bill for someone else to pay after his death, he paid for the ambulance that took him to the hospital on the very day he died. He left an honest name for his children and a good example of liberality to follow.

COMMUNITY LIFE

Although our community life pivoted around the church, during the week the older children went to school at Dry Prong and the younger ones went to a little two-room school house in the Prospect community. Mrs. Mae Bell taught three grades in one room while another teacher taught the forth and fifth grades in the other. We must have been a trial of patience to this poor soul who had known finer things in life before she came into our lives. Nature's children would deliberately take off their shoes and step into the deepest mud holes to see how thick they could form mud boots on their feet so they could then track them into the schoolroom. In spite of all of our country tricks, Mrs. Bell managed to teach us enough to pass us on to higher grades at Dry Prong.

At Dry Prong High School our teachers did their best to prepare us for adult life and present us to the outside world. There our horizons expanded to the rest of our state. We even went as far north as Winnfield and as for south as Baton Rouge on school excursions and literary rallies.

Several of us were valedictorians in our graduating classes (I was not one of these) and went on to be distinguished in higher education. A teacher once remarked to me that there was something different about the children who came from our community. Just what all she meant I don't know, but I sensed she meant it in a good way. Something must have been done very right here plus maybe the DNA stacked up just right for a high IQ in some. This does not deny the fact that there were enough wild genes among us to keep us humble. Lack of an official education on the part of our progenitors did not mean they were unintelligent or that their offspring would be ignoramuses. Certainly none of the younger generation should be ashamed of their ancestors or of their humble beginnings because these, our people, have passed on traits coupled with good upbringing to produce children who have excelled. After all, their children's genes did come from them. Nevertheless, we all had the nature to sin and had we not been born again, by the grace of God, we would have all gone the way of the world.

On the weekends all other activities took a back seat to getting ready for church. Everyone had his weekend bath in water heated outside with our own version of solar heating. If we were fortunate enough, we had a double size galvanized washtub in which to bathe; if not, a single number three would work by doubling up your knees to your chin. In the wintertime we heated the water and placed the tub in front of the fireplace for our baths.

I remember those occasions when we came home from school with the seven-year itch (scabies). We were scrubbed until the skin nearly peeled off after which a generous coating of a paste made with lard and sulfur was applied. On the following morning we were scrubbed again before we went out so as not to smell up the whole schoolroom or church when the temperatures soared. (Believe it or not, the remedy worked.)

Jeannie Montgomery

No one went to church dirty on Sundays, and our houses were always just as clean as we were for the weekend. After our Saturday baths, the bath water had lye added and then sloshed on the floors which were scrubbed to spotless perfection with corn shuck mops. We might have been dirt poor, but never dirty!

Ready for Sunday, our parents welcomed the pastor and his family to spend the weekend in our homes. Many times they ended up staying at our house which had almost become the unofficial parsonage of the church since the pastor did not live in this community. Daddy was a long way from being a preacher, but he was a heavy supporter of the ministry. Preachers felt very much at home with us. That is how I learned Baptist doctrine early in life. I also became acquainted with many of those little idiosyncrasies preachers have which children notice with interest. I never wanted one of them to get serious with me and talk directly to me about my soul's condition, but I was ready in a split second to laugh at anything that was odd or funny which they did.

Once a preacher, who had received his doctorate in a well-known seminary, dropped by to spend the night. Even the best educated person in the world is still ignorant about some things; this brother was no exception. That night he was about to experience one of those "unlearned" moments when a thunderstorm hit with a vengeance. Our house had a tin roof and he had never heard rain beat on such a roof before. The gully washer sounded like God was bent on tearing up the countryside with a devastating hailstorm.

He jumped out of bed in haste and called my Dad, "Come quickly, Bro. Garlington. Let's pray for God to stop this hail. Bro. Enos' turnip patch is going to be ruined."

We believe in praying about everything, but how do you pray for something when you know that God is not going to stop what He never started?

As always, children remember the different and not the usual. Ever since I can remember, Bro. T.L. Blalock, one of the early Baptist missionaries who went to China in the late 1800's, held a special place in my memories. He could hold my attention like a magnet that clings to metal. When old Bro. T. L., dressed in his Chinese clothing, got up to speak at Corinth to share his experiences in China, my imagination went wild. Maybe it was because when he came, we always sang "Footprints of Jesus." Just to hear the first part of the second verse, "Though they lead o'er the cold dark mountains, Seeking His sheep..." was all it took for me to have visions of him struggling up some faraway "cold dark mountain" with, of course, his little Chinese skull cap on his head as he preached to the multitude. Somehow the sun we knew in this part of the world never rose over China, and the people over there were in a cold miserable state. He also carried a pocketful of prunes with him because I saw him eat some of them before he went to bed every night at our house. Yet without his knowing it, and even amid my jumbled up childish visions of a missionary's life on a foreign field, he left an indelible impression on me as to what is right and proper about mission work. The direct contact of churches with the missionary they support is a precious blessing which many modern churches have lost as new methods of spreading the gospel substitute the tried and proven ways of the Apostle Paul. Bro. Blalock practiced what we at Corinth believe and support. Using his terminology it is best known as, "direct faith missions." Being interpreted, each church sends its offerings directly to the missionary on the field, and the missionary on his part has faith that God will supply his every need by the direction of the Holy Spirit. This system, as ancient as it may seem, has never failed those who are really called of God. I would not recommend this to one who is only looking for an adventure or is persuaded by some high strung emotional preacher to go to foreign fields by his misguided zeal.

Although a preacher may be well intentioned, he should be doubly sure God has called him and not man. One's calling must be of God or he is asking for trouble. That principle is still my conviction.

Many other spiritual leaders had a profound mark upon this community. There were those special ones at whom I never dared laugh. As I begin to grow up, their John the Baptist messages of "Repent ye for the kingdom of heaven is at hand," sent me running for cover. I was as lost as the thief on the cross, but I never wanted to admit it to anyone. We knew early in life that just because our families were Christian didn't mean it automatically put us among the saved; neither did joining the church make us sons of God even though we were His creation. Jesus said to Nicodemus, "Ye must be born again." John 3:7. John expressed it just right when he said, "But as many as received him, to them gave he power to become the sons of God, even to them that believe on his name. Which were born, not of blood, nor of the will of the flesh, nor of the will of man, but of God." John 1:14, 15. That meant we couldn't get into heaven by swinging in on our mamas' and papas' coat tails. Something drastic had to happen within our own hearts.

I was petrified the night I realized I was not going to heaven if I died. The elderly evangelist, physically tired from preaching, came over and sat on the piano stool right in front of me to finish his sermon. He knew me by name since he was staying at our house. I trembled because I felt sure he was going to ask me right there in front of a house full of people, if I were saved or not. He swung back and forth on the twirling stool with his accusing finger pointing at the congregation. Dropping my head so he wouldn't pay any attention to me, I thought I would surely miss his finger but, alas, it was not meant to be. Suddenly, he stopped with his finger at my nose.

I wanted to drop through the floor.

"Now I'm in trouble," I thought. "He's going to embarrass me for sure."

Instead he only said, "Jeannie, go get me a fan, please."

What a relief! By that time I needed the fan more than he. He was not about to put a nine-year-old child on the spot, but I felt so guilty I fully expected him to do it anyway. I didn't know that God was calling me to repentance.

It was four years later that I trusted the Lord to save me. My experience of faith is one that somehow I do not get up in public to relate. You see, it all happened in our outdoor toilet. Nevertheless, that day changed my life when I first knelt before Him and in faith believed that He would save me.

Growing up among so many of the church members who were related, it didn't matter where we children sat in church; we were automatically under the supervision of any nearby adult when the services started. In fact, relative or not, all had our parents blessing to give a resounding thump on a deserving child.

The most humiliating situation for any youngster was to have to go sit up in the "Amen Corner" of the church with the elders. No child sat there by choice or because we were little spiritual giants. This corner normally reserved for the men was situated directly to the left of the pulpit and in front of the whole audience. The position itself required perfect comportment on the part of some misbehaving child. I must have sat there quite frequently because I remember clearly when Uncle Mike Cline, who really wasn't an uncle, came to the part of his prayer where he always said, "And at last receive us unto thyself," I knew he was closing out. I could almost tell you in advance what certain brethren were going to say in their memorized prayers. Others preached God a sermon and told God what he already knew. Some seemed to wait until they got to church to get caught up on their praying and did it all at one time. Even so, there was one thing for sure, when a serious problem arose, everybody hit the deck with their knees and knew how to plead with God. We kids sat in reverence and awe without having to be thumped at those times.

On the other side of the pulpit there were several benches where the choir sat. Before the advent of pianos in our community, an old pump organ was put near the choir to accompany them as they sang in harmony from a "Stamps-Baxter" shaped-note song book. Aunt Maggie pumped away with gusto as she accompanied the congregation on those lively, ever changing tunes as well as on the old timeless hymns which remained long after the new editions had come and gone. With modern times came the more modern piano and other hymnals, but we learned to sing by the old shape-note method which Uncle Reecie Honeycutt taught us in singing schools in the summertime.

Music was as necessary for our daily lives as food. The young people enjoyed getting together nearly every Saturday night at one of the parents' homes to sing and drink hot chocolate or eat popcorn. Sadly, the age of wholesome home fun vanished with that generation.

World War II changed our community as it did most of the United States. Our placid innocence was forever lost. We didn't have to go out looking for the world; it came to our front door. Army training camps were built all around us. Our fields and properties became training camps for young soldiers going to war. Mock military battles were fought at our very own front door steps. We didn't complain because our own young men were in training elsewhere. Some of them would never return. Families all dreaded the day when that yellow slip of paper would be brought to the door by a soldier or by some government official.

One morning only a few hours after Daddy had left for work, he returned. He staggered to the gatepost and hung on to keep from falling. The dreaded little yellow slip was in his hand. He did not have to say a word. We all knew. My brother Tim was not ever coming home again.

TIMOTHY O'DONALD GARLINGTON

Tim was eager to join the army. When he graduated from high school he was not quite 18, but he persuaded Dad to sign for him to get in right away. The day Dad carried him to Camp Beauregard to leave him, I went along.

There were at least two newspaper articles written about Tim's bravery in Italy, but what I cherish most is the visit his buddy made us after the war was over. He told how Tim had died peacefully. He couldn't understand the calm with which Tim went, but we did. Tim had trusted the Savior before he went into war and was not afraid of dying.

When Tim left for the war, I think Mama knew Tim would never return home to us again. I overheard Daddy say he was praying that if one of his sons in service must die to let it be Tim since Nathan had two small children. I only tell this so that I can say what my heart has cried out over the years. Don't give God an "either-or" prayer to answer. "Open your mouth wide," God said to Israel, "and I will fill it."

After Tim's death, Mother's health went into a steady decline ultimately bringing on the end of her life. Those were difficult times. I was thrown into the role of being mother to my younger sister and housekeeper for my Dad and brother, Leonard. My other brothers and sisters were either married or working away from home. The things that I could not thank God for when they happened, later became a heart-felt prayer of thanksgiving when I had to use the hard learned lessons from those days. Truly, "...all things work together for good to them that love God, to them who are the called according to his purpose."

I could not begin to give a full account of all my relatives but they all had a special place in my growing up and were part of preparing me for my yet unknown future.

Chapter Two
Off to Japan

Home on a weekend pass from nursing school, I was captivated by the overactive child jumping around me in front of the fireplace. Fiction was as true to him as fact in the wild tale he spun about a Japan he was yet to see.

"One day," he began, "when I was climbing up Mt. Fuji, a big black bear came running after me." Then trying to give credence to his story he ended by saying, "And I ran with patience the race that was set before me."

Little Tommy's mixture of imagination with the scriptures made me laugh; but had I known that in a little over a year I would be standing beside this very child within plain view of Mt. Fuji, my reaction might have been another. While his bear was imaginary, the old snow capped volcano was for real, and the race that was set before me would take a lifetime of patience.

With the coming of his missionary parents, John and Mary Blalock, to our church, my life was about to make a drastic change. While Tommy talked freely, Bro. John was quietly thoughtful. Later I found out that for some reason, he thought that I would make a good wife for his young missionary friend, Steve Montgomery, who was also going to Japan. He resolved to tell him about me and to recommend that our church invite Steve to come preach. Thank goodness he didn't say anything to me because I would have turned him off right then. For a preacher to have a department store name like Montgomery somehow made him a strange human being beyond my realm of interest. However, our church did invite Steve to come by on his way to Japan.

STEVE HAROLD MONTGOMERY

By the time Steve came through our church doors for the first time in September of 1953, I had already formed a strong negative opinion about him. Everyone including the pastor had told me that I was going to marry this unknown missionary, and that irritated me considerably. It wasn't that I didn't want to be a missionary's wife because I had always wanted to be. I just didn't want other people deciding for me what I thought was only the Lord's business and mine.

Seeing his reflected image in a nearby window as he entered that night, I grunted to myself, "Huh, I'll never marry that thing."

God has a way of changing things. Something inside me began to stir when Steve began to sing and speak. I sat up and paid attention. Here was a man with a cultured musical talent and one who had a formidable command of the Bible that he delivered in almost impeccable grammar.

Before he finished, I said another, "Huh," to myself but with less irritation. "Maybe I should at least pray about this guy." It never crossed my mind that Steve might have something to say about the matter, too.

Since Bro. John failed to tell him my name, Steve was still in the dark about who I was. The seventeen or so young girls in the church only confused him. Being timid around girls, he left without knowing which one was the student Nurse John had told him about.

These My People

After he left, I prayed an odd prayer, "Lord, please help Steve find my good friend in Monroe; she will make him a good wife. But, Lord, if you want me to marry him, then let him come back to Corinth."

At nearly every place Steve went after he left Corinth, he was asked, "Did you meet Jeannie?"

He began to wonder who this "Jeannie" was. His curiosity peaked when he visited Bro. T. N. Davis, an elderly ex-pastor of Corinth. Oddly enough, Steve did not have a preaching appointment that weekend, so the pastor suggested they make another visit to Corinth. Bro. Davis brought him straight to our house. I was home for the weekend, which made it convenient for us to get to know each other. When Steve saw my nursing books, he realized that Jeannie and the girl John had told him about were one and the same person. Evidently some things are meant to be, and our marriage was one of those things.

From that point on, life took on a fast pace for me; and before I knew it, I was on my way to Japan as Mrs. Steve Montgomery. That is when I really began to know the man that I married.

One of the first things I learned was that I was not first in his life; God was. That was the way I wanted it.

The next thing I learned was that if he were in the middle of preachers, he forgot that he had a wife. That took awhile for me to get use to, but I did come to understand that fellowship with his colleagues was like energy flowing through his veins which he needed.

He could make a fairly accurate snap judgment of a person or situation that had its advantages and disadvantages.

There were times when he was very stern, and others when he was very entertaining.

Steve rarely found himself without words. Without a doubt his ability to articulate well, coupled with his wonderful ear for music made him an excellent linguist. However his forte was the ability to teach in simple terms the doctrines of the Bible, which is an absolute necessity if a missionary desires to leave a church in condition to be autonomous. This was one of God's greatest gifts to him, and no doubt was the reason God called him to go to other lands.

Although I have seen Steve faint at the sight of blood, he has had an uncanny God given strength to face danger even when his life was at stake. He was not one to back off from a bad situation; so much so, there were times I feared for him. I was the scaredy-cat, not Steve.

After fifty-four years I can read him like the palm of my hand, but most things are for only me to read. I can say that he has always wanted to do God's will, and there has never been any manipulating scheme on his part to obtain anything in this life. If God did not grant him his desires, he didn't want it. In spite of any fault he might have had, I know that he had rather die than not to serve God. This was the man that I married.

After we were married, we did have a few mishaps on our way to Japan. In Chicago nearly everything we owned was stolen. Just because a person is dedicated to serving God doesn't exempt him from having problems. On the contrary, many times he has to suffer like the apostle Paul, who was in constant danger everywhere he went. Our little trouble was nothing compared to his but God had a good purpose in letting it happen. I think most of the blame lies on me. Before we got married, I had purchased some very nice clothing and was becoming a little vain about it. When I realized what I was doing, I asked God to forgive me and take them away if that was what I needed. As soon as I had prayed that prayer, I promptly forgot it and only remembered it the night all our things were stolen. Our passports and everything inside the car were gone. I felt so guilty that I confessed to Steve what I had prayed. He didn't know what to do with me. Not only were all of my clothes gone but so were his.

These My People

"For goodness sake, the next time you pray, warn me," he burst out. Then in a calmer mood he added, "But I am glad I married a woman God hears when she prays."

We had to get our documents all over again as fast as possible because our sailing date was fast approaching. Some of Steve's old friends had told him that we could not go to Japan as missionaries with only our local church's approval. They proved to be wrong because we not only got our entrance visa once but twice! God is head over all things *for the church*; and when He sends a person, He can handle all the details. Nevertheless, our faith was put to the test until the day before we sailed. We got our new visas just in time to step on board the Japanese ship, Hikawa Maru, May 1, 1954 in Seattle, Washington.

If ever there were a forlorn, tear-jerking sound, Hikawa Maru's foghorn certainly takes the preeminence over all. Besides the horn's long, "Faaawnk" of doom, the loud speaker was squeaking out a rendition of "Auld Lang Syne" that sounded like our deaths were imminent. Caught up in the emotion of the moment, my spirit was completely in tune with the music. Watching all that I had ever known as home began to disappear as the waters of Puget Sound came rushing in between my homeland and me, I felt that my roots had been yanked up and washed out to sea. A sense of desolation set in. What would the future hold for us so completely separated from home?

When my cousin Nelda and I were children, we tried to cross her daddy's cow pond in a washtub. We had barely shoved off when the tub over turned in knee-deep water. That aborted attempt at sailing had not prepared me for the high seas. Everything was foreign to me; even my husband was almost a stranger. Words cannot express the blessedness of having the One, who holds the land and sea in His hands, right by your side at these times.

Jeannie Montgomery

Not everybody on the ship shared my morbid sentiments. Some were glad to be going home to Japan. Down the hall from us we could hear an old Japanese man singing everyday. The music was totally different from anything I had ever heard. Each note started out as a deep guttural groan and ended somehow with a sad nasal twang. I couldn't understand a word he was singing, but I sensed that the man was giving in to pent-up emotions he had constrained while in a foreign land. Now that he was going home, his crying song was that of returning not of leaving.

Pacific is a misnomer for the Northern Pacific Ocean. A few days out from Seattle, a storm hit our ship with almost hurricane force. We were tossed in every direction a ship can go without going down. Mountains of water swelled up in front of us only to fling us down the next moment on the other side with avalanche force. No one dared go out on the decks. The mighty waves could have easily washed us overboard. If we ventured out of our bunks into the hall, we hung onto rails to keep from falling. Most of the passengers got seasick. Those who didn't laughed at those who did. The dining room was almost always empty. Everyone had a remedy for seasickness; some said it was all in your head. In a few days we didn't care which we needed, a medical doctor or a psychiatrist. Just go get one. This went on for most of the seventeen days we were at sea. When the storm finally subsided, we were only a couple of days from Japan. The air became heavy with an old musky smell. I heard someone say, "Do you smell that odor? That is Japan."

From then on we spent most of our time out on the deck looking for land. Our long and rough trip was finally over when we docked May 17, 1954, in Yokohama, Japan.

CHAPTER THREE
JAPAN 1954-1957

ONE OF THE SWEETEST SIGHTS a person can see after a perilous journey is a familiar face waiting on the docks. Steve and I were both very green and not at all travel wise. Our God knew this so he sent the Blalocks to greet and comfort us.

Nearly nine years after the end of World War II, we stepped into a Japan still struggling to rise out of its devastating ruins. Official military occupation had ended on April 28, 1952; but there still remained much to be done. Progress had not yet given Japan its modern look of today. As far as the eye could see, a never ending chain of old dilapidated, unpainted, wooden buildings seemed to join each other wall to wall. The narrow streets were lined with open sewer ditches. Adding to the overall picture of dullness and poverty were the steady streams of drably clad people milling in the streets. My first impression was people, people everywhere. Where did they all come from? Where were those picture postcard places I had seen?

While John and Steve took care of our baggage, Mary took me to their house in a taxi. From the way our driver drove, I decided that he must have been a frustrated kamikaze pilot who didn't have the chance to sacrifice himself in the war but was bent on fulfilling his mission with us in the car. He sped down the narrow streets without slowing for anything. Chickens, dogs, and human beings alike flew out of his way. Was I ever relieved when we came to a safe stop in front of the Blalock's house!

The Blalock's house was just another one in the endless chain of old buildings. All of the houses were spilling over with people crowded into small areas much like tiny circus cars. With our arrival their house was full, too. Even so, they very graciously opened their home to us for two weeks before we found a house in Tokyo.

From the beginning Bro. John began to introduce oriental food to us. One of his favorites was *O-tofu,* a soybean curd which he scrambled with eggs. Due to the ground fish meal the farmers fed their chickens, the eggs tasted like fish. Therefore, everything a body puts eggs in, from breakfast food to desserts, definitely tasted fishy. It took some adjusting to get used to it. I thought his first breakfast tasted very much like I imagined fish and eggs scrambled in castor oil would be.

Bro. John was an interesting person. Besides his playing a part in our own lives, there is a great story behind this man.

JOHN BLALOCK

As a young single missionary in the last part of the 1930's, John went to China to work with his Uncle T. L. Blalock in the Baptist China Direct Mission. He was there when the Japanese invaded and took control of part of China. In 1940 the relations between the U.S. and Japan became so tense until all the missionaries were told to flee the country. They were in extreme danger. He was entrusted with the responsibility of getting three American children born of a Chinese mother and an American father, who had died, out of China to the United States. They were in danger for being half American. He managed to get them out of the country with him as far as the

Philippine Islands before war broke out between Japan and the United States. A month later, in January of 1942, the Japanese took control of the Philippines; and they were taken captive along with a large number of other American missionaries. For three years they suffered in the prison camps with many of them dying from hunger and untreated diseases. John and the three children survived the ordeal by God's mercy and were among those who were liberated in February of 1945. He wrote his intriguing story in his book, "Through Fire and Through Water."

After the Chinese communists ran the Japanese out, Bro. John could not return to his beloved mission. Instead he decided to go to Japan when the war was over. During the time he was preparing to go, he married Mary. When they came to my parents' house in the spring of 1953 on their way to Japan, they had two small children. His prison ordeal had not taken away his love for lost souls, even for those who had been his captors.

Bro. John had some extraordinarily difficult trials in his life that took him off the foreign mission field, but his heart still remains there until now. Through all of his struggles, he never faltered, but always remained an inspiration to others. Although there are hundreds of people in other lands today that do not know him, they came to know the Lord partly because of the influence Bro. John had on the missionary's life. Steve and I are privileged to know this man.

After two weeks we left the Blalock's warm home to move to Tokyo where we planned to enter the Naganuma language school. With our fellow companions, the Fords, we rented a house until we could get better situated.

As soon as we could, we opened our house for church services on Sundays. Out of necessity the services were first held in English. As a result of this, we attracted several young men who were more interested in learning English than in learning the Bible, but after awhile some of them genuinely became interested in hearing more about Jesus and made professions of faith. Most were either of high school or college age. Because Japan had lost the war, many young people lost faith in their traditional religions and were open minded to hear the Gospel. This was a golden era for spreading the Gospel.

Soon we had several young men who said that they believed and wanted to be baptized. These young men had never seen a Baptist baptism so didn't know what to expect. As it turned out, we were the ones who had the surprise waiting for us. Green missionaries that we were, we failed to advise them about what clothing they were to carry to the river. When we all arrived there, we had our brief preaching service before the preacher led them into the water for the symbolic burial. Then just before stepping into the water, the young men began to take off their clothing. When they got down to their underwear, the missionaries caught them in time. They were the first ever and, I might add, the last new believers to be baptized in nothing but their long johns.

Before we left Japan there were around thirty-five young men in the church. A couple of these I remember very well.

YASUDA SAN

Yasuda was one of the first to come into our church. Through his influence many others came to hear the Gospel. He was a good person who looked after the welfare of his fellow peers. One day as he was crossing a bridge on foot, he saw a young girl about to jump into the river to commit suicide. Persuading her not to jump, he brought her to our house so we could talk to her about the Lord. When it came time for her to go, she didn't want to leave. We didn't know what to do because evidently she was a minor, and we thought that her parents would be worrying about her by then. We couldn't put her out on the streets so we just let her spend the night. The next two days it was the same story; she didn't want to go home. Finally, Yasuda said, "That's enough."

He made her leave and took her to her father's house where he told everything that had transpired. Her father just shrugged his shoulders, not caring one bit what had happened to his daughter. Yasuda had handled the situation like a Christian man should. He grew about a foot spiritually that day in my eyes.

We could always depend on him.

KOMATSU SAN

Several months after we had moved to Tokyo, Steve and I rented a house in another part of the town near the language school where we were enrolled. One evening a young man came to our door with a well-worn Bible in his hand. Unlike so many who came only to learn English, he came because he really wanted us to explain the Word to him. He was greatly disturbed about his life. By that time Steve could carry on a limited conversation in Japanese, but it was still difficult to explain well how a person could be saved. Komatsu San knew some English so between the two they were able to find the right scriptures for him to read about salvation. They finished their study with a prayer. Since praying in another language is very difficult for anyone who is learning that language, Steve prayed in English.

When Steve finished his prayer, Komatsu asked, "Can God understand if I pray in Japanese?"

"Of course," Steve reassured him. "God created all the languages and he can hear in any language."

Komatsu knelt beside our couch, dropped his head and prayed. I couldn't understand what he said, but I did understand the tears and smile that were on his face when he looked up.

A couple of years later when we were boarding the Hikawa Maru to leave Japan, I was very touched when I saw him cry. Only God can make people of such different cultures love one another.

For several years we kept in touch with him, but later lost knowledge of his whereabouts. We do know that he went to college in Japan and won a scholarship to study in England where he got his doctorate degree. He also went to Russia; then later taught in the University of Tokyo. When he got married, he wrote us a letter asking our blessings on his marriage. We lost contact for many years but only recently established contact again. .

I often wonder if he still remembers that God can hear a Japanese pray in his own language.

While we still lived in the Naganuma School area, we began to venture out and experiment the local cuisine. We had learned in school that *sukiyaki* was one of the more famous of the national dishes, so we wanted to try it. Steve asked a neighbor where was the best place to find it. Thinking that Steve was like most Japanese men who have a night out on the town, our neighbor indicated a walled in compound not too far from our house within easy walking distance. Neither of us knew what we were getting into. When we went through the gates, we could see the main building at the center of a large number of small buildings around it. In the main house a woman took our order and ushered us to one of the smaller houses. Inside we watched with interest as the kimono clad woman prepared our meal in a wok over a burner set on the low table where we ate with our legs doubled up under us. All the time back behind us another young woman sat demurely on the rice straw floor, grinning and bowing. I would grin and bow back. She never said a word the whole time we were there. After the meal was over, I thought Steve was going to burst a blood vessel when he saw the bill! He was charged with the "use" of the grinning geisha. Somehow he let the old lady who controlled everything know that he would not pay for anything but our food. We got out of there in a hurry, but we did carry with us one thing besides a lesson learned. From that day on I could really cook a mean sukiyaki when I wanted to.

Another event helped us to know in what kind of neighborhood we were living; it made us want to move. As we were walking down the sidewalk, we passed a woman on my side of the walk. All of a sudden Steve caught my arm and said, "Honey, she pinched me." She had reached behind me to pinch him. It was time to move.

There is another incident of this nature which happened to me that shows why I believe a young single woman should not go to a foreign mission field. When we moved to another area, we had to take two trains to go to church. One night as we were returning, we boarded a train that was loaded almost to capacity. The benches were lined up on either side facing the middle. In the middle people stood hanging onto swinging straps above us. We managed to find me a seat between two ladies, but Steve only found one on the opposite side a little distance away. At the next station the ladies got up at the same time to get off. Immediately two men standing in front of me plopped down on either side and grabbed me by both arms. Evidently they had not seen Steve until he came alive in front of them. Steve completely forgot what Japanese he knew and yelled at them in English to let me go. It didn't take a linguist to know what he was saying. Dropping my arms, the men jumped up and left in a hurry.

My advice to any young well-meaning woman who wants to be a missionary is to get married to a missionary. God will provide you a husband if He wants you to go to the mission field. It's not a bad idea either for the young men to be married before they go. I shudder to think what would have happened to me if Steve had not been there.

We were renting one end of a house owned by a wartime widow who had divided her home so she could live in one end and rent the other. Evidently her husband, a high ranking officer in the Japanese army, left her a nice but old style house. Sliding doors opened into a backyard full of miniature *bonsai* plants placed among little oriental light stands. Overall, it was pleasant to live in these surroundings.

While we were living here, our first child, David, was born. Not knowing of a hospital close at hand, we went to the Seventh Day Adventist hospital across town for his birth. The nightmare most mothers fear almost happened to me two days after his birth. I could hear a baby crying in a patient's room down the hall. Instinctively, I knew it was David; but why was his cry coming from that room? I jumped up and ran to the room. After asking permission to come in, I asked to see the woman's baby. The lady, who was getting her twins ready to leave for home, had just about finished packing and was ready to go. I picked up the arm of one of the babies, and sure enough, Montgomery was written on his arm beads. When I showed the woman the name, she was confused. She said, "I thought something was strange, but forgive me, I do have two babies."

Isn't it marvelous how God made David cry at the right time and how I knew it was he even though I had seen him only a few times since he was born? Believe me, Steve and I were two happy and thankful parents to be taking home our very own baby.

Everything went well between our landlady and us until soon after we carried David home; then something unusual happened. We had placed his baby bed in a nook called a *tokonoma* which the Japanese usually reserve for wall hangings and religious objects. It was a perfect place for his bed. One morning we woke up to see that a big carved log from over his head had fallen down, barely missing David. It was lying across the headboard of the baby bed! Steve and I were thankful God had spared our baby, but we thought it best to tell our landlord what happened. Visibly shaken, she snatched up the log, hugged it to herself, and hurried off to the next room without saying anything about how wonderful it was that David was not hit. A little later she came back with the news that we had to move.

We believe that God makes our changes for us, so we moved once more to another neighborhood. This time it was in a very nice section of town where many well educated people lived. Still we did not know anything about our neighbors. There must have been someone who lived nearby that didn't like our presence. One night we had rocks thrown at us, and on different occasions someone defecated in front of our gate. Americans apparently were not very welcome there. After all, it was only a few years after the Second World War!

By the time we moved, Steve was getting eager to preach in Japanese without the help of a translator. His first attempt at preaching was interesting. We had been so busy we had completely forgotten that it was Mother's Day. We invited everybody we could to come to our Sunday morning services in our living room, which soon filled up with kids and several adults.

Trying to start on an easy level with the kids, Steve asked them if they knew what day it was.

"Mother's Day," they all yelled.

That wasn't quiet the response Steve was expecting. He wanted them to say, "It's Sunday." I guess it must have messed up his line of thought enough to make him flub up in the language, but I didn't know it. I was so proud of him for preaching in Japanese until I thought that he preached with perfection. (Who was I to judge if his Japanese were right or not?)

Among those who attended was a Christian neighbor who was an Ambassador's wife. By the time we were to leave Japan, this lady and I were good friends; and we were able to laugh together about Steve's first sermon.

She said, "Mr. Steve has really improved his ability to speak. You remember that first time he tried to preach in Japanese? Well, I didn't understand a thing."

Other women in our neighborhood also were nice to me. Once a lady wanted me to go with her to an open-air market which was much like a flea market stretched out for blocks. Table after table of nothing but used navy blue or black clothing was not interesting to me. About half way through our shopping, she decided to treat me to a bowl of noodles. Motioning for me to follow, she took me into a little tent where she ordered us a steaming bowl of noodle soup, O-*Soba*, and a couple of raw eggs. Not knowing what she was going to do with the eggs, I just watched as she broke one into my bowl. The only thing I could do was to stir it up good and hope I wouldn't gag when I ate it. Everyone around us was slurping loudly as the noodles slid down their throats. Since that seemed to be the right thing to do, I just joined in with the crowd and gave them my best slurp.

This same woman had Steve and me over for tea one afternoon. She kept us entertained by telling stories of her life. Since I was pregnant with our second child at the time, I remember very vividly how she cupped up her hand to her mouth like a funnel and said, "When I was expecting my children, I craved raw rice. I would take a handful of it and guzzle it down." I wondered if she had to swallow pebbles, too, to grind it up as chickens do in their craw and gizzards!

Shortly before David was born, my formal language schooling ended. From then on I was on my own if I wanted to learn more. I became very adept at listening and trying to associate one thing with

These My People

another. Besides his regular classes Steve also had a tutor come to our house to help him learn Bible terms. As he became more efficient in the language, I also began to understand more of what was being said. Speaking the language came to me later.

My heart went out to Steve's young teacher. He was not coming to our house because he was curious about us or because he liked us. He was extremely bitter against Americans. His sole purpose in coming was to make a living. During the war he lost an ear and some of his fingers were deformed from being burned by the atom bomb dropped on Nagasaki. (In all my travels I have yet to meet a foreigner who remembers that the Americans are the ones who had bombs first dropped on them. What they do remember is that Americans are the ones who committed the "terrible atrocity" of dropping the atom bomb. They never think that in spite of all the damage done, in the long run there were more lives saved by dropping it. The horror of that awful moment is engraved in their minds and has molded their attitude toward the Americans).

The amazing power of the Gospel is the only thing that can soften and change a bitter heart. As Steve and the young teacher studied together, this victim of the atom bomb began to lose his resentment against Christians. He began to listen to what Jesus had to say. In time he began to attend our meetings. Before we left Japan, our enemy had become our friend.

One day when Steve was downtown, a popular photography magazine display caught his eye. There was a beautiful picture of a baptismal service being performed in the ocean near Hiroshima. Looking closely he saw that it was our friend, Bro. James Smith, who had started a church in that area and was baptizing new converts. By this time Steve could read enough Japanese characters to know what the author said. The author knew nothing about Christianity but said that he was greatly moved by this ceremony because evidently it meant that the person being baptized was symbolically dying to the way he had lived and was being raised to live a new life. Isn't it amazing that God left us such a clear picture in the form of baptism that even someone who had not been taught doctrine knew exactly what it means?

Because my health was precarious before our second son Timothy was born, we had to arrange for household help. The young Christian girl who came to live with us was one of the first persons in Japan to mention Brazil to us. Her uncle had gone there as an immigrant because opportunities were opening up for Japanese to settle in that country. At that time things were so bad in Japan, they were leaving in large numbers. Large passenger ships were loaded with immigrants going to Brazil constantly. One such ship was named the Brazil Maru. It was odd how we constantly encountered someone going to Brazil.

Shortly after Timothy was born, the girl received a letter from her uncle. When she read it, she looked at us with tears in her eyes and said, "If I were a missionary, I would go to Brazil because my people leave one kind of idolatry here only to go into another kind there." She then turned to Steve and asked, "Why don't you go?"

Without saying anything to anyone or to each other, Steve and I both began to think and pray about going to Brazil. It seemed so foolish because we were just becoming comfortable in the language and in knowing how to get around. There was a great need for the gospel where we were. A few months passed, and one night Steve woke up and could not go back to sleep. I sensed he was awake and worried about something so I asked, "What's bothering you? Are you thinking about going to Brazil?"

He was shocked that I asked him that because I hit the nail right on the head. We prayed about it together right then and agreed to wait on the Lord to show us what to do. Many things began to happen very

These My People

soon, and all of our prayers were answered in regards to our going. What really clenched our decision was an answer to a prayer we made during a meeting we were holding in a rented hall near our house. Conversions are rather scarce in Japan, but we asked God that if He wanted us to go to Brazil to work that someone would be saved that night in our services. Steve did not preach that night but sat with me out in the audience. When the preacher gave the invitation, no one moved. It looked like we were staying in Japan; but after the final amen was said, a young girl sitting right behind us turned to Steve and asked, "How may I be saved?" Quickly everyone gathered around as we told her the simple story of the death, burial and resurrection of Jesus to save us from our sins.

When she heard the story of Jesus' grace, she said she believed. She was the daughter of a Buddhist monk. She only came a few times after this and I feel sure that her family would not let her come, but God had answered our prayer about going to Brazil. We began to make arrangements to leave Japan. We had told no one in America of this struggle and our decision that was so hard to make; but without knowing the special need, several churches sent us enough money to return to the United States. Getting an entrance visa into Brazil was easy also.

After making all the necessary arrangements for leaving, we again boarded the Hikawa Maru to go back to Seattle, Washington. As our crepe paper streamers from us to our people on the dock began to snap as we slipped away from the shore, a chapter in our lives was completed. This time the sadness I felt was that of leaving a group with which we had worked and had seen God change their lives. It was very much like a mother leaving her baby.

Back on the ocean again, a few days out, our ship captain received word that a typhoon was headed directly in our path. All the passengers

Jeannie Montgomery

were warned of the trouble ahead so we would be prepared. If going to Japan had been rough, what would this be like? Steve and I went to our room and knelt before the Master of the Seas. To Him who can change the course of the storm, we pleaded for Him to do just that and left it in His hands. The next morning word came that the storm would miss us but we would have some turbulent seas.

    I am thankful we serve a God who answers prayer!

CHAPTER FOUR
GETTING PRIORITIES STRAIGHT
1957

THE INTENSITY WITH WHICH I had lived the past three years caved in on me when the children and I reached Steve's parents' home in Texarkana, Arkansas. Steve had sent us home by plane while he visited several supporting churches on the way south. On our voyage to Japan, the old man who sang every morning had a song to express his feelings about going home, but I had none. I just sat down and cried.

Someone asked, "What's the matter?"

I couldn't answer. How could I say, "Do you know what it's like to be away from family love? to be in danger on land and sea? to be sick in a foreign land where you have two babies and an operation with only strangers around? to learn another language? to adapt to another culture? to boil every drop of your drinking water? to sterilize every bite of food you eat? to keep going with your husband on his missions in spite of being physically weak? to learn to love a strange people you must later leave? and then to come to a safe haven where all stress is gone?" I could no more express that than a soldier could tell about all of his bottled up emotions when he comes home from combat. Tears were my unutterable words and I said a bucket full.

After I had rested a few days and my babies had time to be with their grandparents, my sister Esther and her husband Murwyn came to take us to Louisiana. There was strangeness about going back "home" after I had been away so long. Observing everybody, I perceived that life on the home front was carried on right well without me. A twinge of disappointment hit me as I realized I wasn't so terribly missed, certainly not as much as I had missed them. I wanted to be cuddled and pampered as if I had been a vital part of community life. Once I heard a missionary say that he was like Abraham going to a far country to live and never return. Inside me I secretly told God, "That's he talking; I'm not that spiritual. I want to go where you want me to go; but, please, dear Lord, let me go back to see my folk every once in awhile. I need my people."

I had to come to terms with God again as we prepared to go to Brazil. Going to Japan we went with such sweet ignorant bliss. On this our second mission trip I knew the stark reality of what lay ahead. I recalled that just before Steve and I married, a preacher I didn't even know came up to me at a funeral, pointed his finger in my face and gave me this stern warning; "Young lady, I want you to know that, when you get to Japan, you are going to suffer."

Confused at the moment that a preacher would say such a thing, I perceived that his heart felt desire was that I would suffer. Immediately, God's gentle Word soothed his jab. "For I reckon that the sufferings of this present time are not worthy to be compared with the glory which shall be revealed in us." Looking back, I had to admit to myself that if he were praying for me to suffer, his prayer was answered. Yes, I had suffered, but thank God there is a wonderful side to the story, too, without which we should have stayed at home. For whatever reason this prophet of doom had in pronouncing his sentence, he failed to see that "in all these things we are more than conquerors through him that loved us," Romans. 8:37. Even walking in the midst of trouble, we had helped start a new church, had seen young people turn to the true God, had learned a language that would help us in another land, had seen God take care of us, and had learned how to do mission work and how not to do it. All of that outweighed any hardship we might have gone through. Truly, God had given us the victory. Nevertheless, the intruding element of doubt cropped up at any opportune chance I gave it.

After hearing glowing reports of a biography of Adoniram Judson, I felt I should read the book. Instead of encouraging some lonely, struggling missionary, the story had the opposite effect on me. All I could see was Judson's three dead wives lying in their dismal graves in a foreign land. Even old Bro. T. L. Blalock, whom I held in high esteem, was no comfort to me in this respect; he himself had buried two wives and had married the third. The odds seemed to be three to one against me living a normal life span. Did missionary life wear out wives three times faster than it did men? It surely looked that way to me. There was absolutely nothing romantic about heading up the list of young brides that Steve would bury; I wanted to live and work with him.

The next question was: "But are you willing to lay down your life for the Lord?" This was the real battle in my heart.

One thing that I never doubted was the will of God for me to marry Steve. Now that we were a family, my place was definitely with my husband wherever he went. That fact stabilized my mind, but I still asked myself a hundred questions. Had not God cared for me in a wonderful way in Japan? Does God only care for Christians on American soil? What if I argued that I loved my children too much to put them in harm's way by taking them to remote places? Would God remove my excuse for not going by taking my children home to Himself if I refused because of them? Was not my love for the Lord supposed to be as great as that of my husband? Jesus had said, "He that loveth father or mother more than me is not worthy of me: and he that loveth son or daughter more than me is not worthy of me. He that taketh not his cross, and followeth after me, is not worthy of me. He that findeth his life shall lose it: and he that loseth his life for my sake shall find it." Matthew. 10:37-39. Where was my dedication to the Lord?

All the time I was questioning myself, in the back of my mind I knew I loved the Lord and wanted to serve Him. I had to come to the point of saying with Job, "Though he slay me, yet will I trust him."

My definition of "home" was changed. Home is where God wants me to be.

I am convinced that a missionary should stay off the field if his wife does not share the same love for the work that he has. If she doesn't, there will be trouble. God doesn't call one to the field without calling his mate to go with him.

Whatever we give up in this life to serve God, he gives back a hundred fold in many ways. Although I would be leaving my biological family, my spiritual family was about to take quantum leaps. During the time we were in the States, two other families, the Rosses and the Rogers, surrendered to go as missionaries to Brazil also. Although they could not go for another year, this meant we would not be alone. We could all lean on each other until we got things going, and this was a big encouragement.

Another little Montgomery came into our lives before we left. Our only American born child, Deborah Jean, was added to our passport. We were finally ready to go to our new destination.

CHAPTER FIVE
GETTING STARTED IN BRAZIL
1958-1960

STEADILY CLIMBING OUT OF THE sweltering Santos Dumont airport in Rio de Janeiro, Brazil, the old DC-4, a World War II relic whose pressurization system did not work, proudly lifted its nose toward the powder puff clouds above us. The gentle bouncing of the plane told us that we had reached our desired altitude, which was cloud level. At this height we could still stay alive without freezing or without dying from the lack of oxygen. The plane gained sufficient altitude to cross Brazil's 2,500 ft. high coastal mountain range by circling out over *Guanabara* Bay and around the world famous statue of Christ the Redeemer situated on *Corcovado* Mountain on our route to São Paulo. Before landing we couldn't help but wonder where our future home lay out there under all the maze of red tile roofs we saw as we flew low over the outskirts of São Paulo. Our three years of experience in Japan had confirmed our belief in Jesus' promise that "when he putteth forth his own sheep, he goeth before them." He had cared for us there and would do so here. Nevertheless, going into a foreign country without knowing a soul or the language posed a tremendous number of challenges we had

Jeannie Montgomery

to meet, not the least of these being, where were we going to sleep with our three babies that night?

In most international airports around the world, there is someone who can speak English; but after you step out on the streets, you plunge immediately into a sea of jumbled up sounds and confusion. How I have often longed in times like these to have the true gift of tongues as they had on the day of Pentecost when they could speak the languages of a different people without having studied it! Since we didn't have that gift and, incidentally, no one else I have ever seen on the mission field has, we had to guess at what was being said. But it was not too hard to deduct that the taxi sign on a car was indeed that of a taxi; so we piled in without knowing where to go. The driver mumbled a number of unintelligible words and finally said something that sounded like "Hotel São Paulo."

Steve nodded his head and repeated, "Hotel São Paulo."

Bravo! We had learned one Portuguese word by the time we had gotten into the car! It worked! Hotel in one language was hotel in the other. The taxi driver carried us straight downtown and left us at the front door of the hotel where we spent our first three nights in Brazil before moving into a more economical one.

When Steve ventured out the next day to get the lay of the land, there were times he felt like unrolling a big ball of twine as he went so he could find his way back. São Paulo is a very complicated place for a native and much more for a foreigner. Seeing a number of Japanese on the street, he tried to get information from them but they were skittish of him and wouldn't answer. They evidently thought he was trying to pull some kind of joke on them since he wasn't oriental.

Before we left Japan we fully intended to work mostly with Japanese. Many who heard that we were going to Brazil gave us names and addresses of relatives and friends to look up when we arrived.

These My People

Fortunately, not too far from our hotel, we found one of these, a Japanese merchant who proved to be a Godsend. Very graciously, he introduced us to a man who arranged for us to stay in a Japanese hotel where we could at least converse with the owners until we could find a house. This man went out of his way to help us. After two weeks in this hotel, we settled in Cidade Leonor, which was located in the general area of Jabaquara on the edge of São Paulo. Touched that we had come to Brazil to work with the Japanese immigrants, our new friend wanted to help us find furniture and whatever else was necessary to set up housekeeping, even though he was not a Christian. He haggled very successfully over the prices at the store where we bought enough used furniture to get by and which served us well for many years. We are extremely indebted to this kind stranger. Truly God has many ways of taking care of His own.

One of the first things we had to do was get a post office box since it would be our lifeline to the outside world. God must have a special sense of humor because only He could have arranged the funny situation that resulted in our getting one quickly. Normally a person could not walk into the downtown post office and come out with a key the same day. He would have to get on a waiting list for months or even years. God knew we needed it immediately and how He would expedite the matter for us. Thinking that a couple of men in the Post Office were Japanese, Steve walked up to them and asked in Japanese if they would translate for him when he applied for a box. They were Chinese! One of them spoke Japanese but not Portuguese and the other could not speak Japanese but could speak Portuguese. So Steve spoke in Japanese to Chinese number 1, who then spoke in Chinese to Chinese number 2, who in turn spoke to the postal employee in Portuguese. The postal employee then sent the answer back in reverse until it got to Steve. This haggling went on for sometime and many postal workers and bystanders gathered around to watch the show and have a good laugh. Steve was given a box within a couple of days, which was record speed! And what a blessing it was to all of us missionary families for many years. It was our lifeline to our brethren back in America.

Thank the Lord we were fluent in the Japanese language. At that time there were around 400,000 Japanese living in São Paulo, a city of 3,500,000 people (the population of Greater São Paulo is said to be over 15,000,000 now). Most of them had been extremely poor in Japan when the Brazilian government opened its doors to Japanese immigrants. Knowing how to be frugal they did quite well as merchants and farmers and many were able to give their children a higher education. Many of them became doctors and pharmacists as well as other professionals. Because we spoke their language, we were able to buy our daily necessities for survival.

Supermarkets were introduced to Brazil in 1957 but were still unheard of where we lived. Instead, there were stores for every different kind of item: the bakery, the vegetable store, the butcher shop, the dry goods store, various others and then twice a week there was the "*Feira*" where everything is sold in open air markets or under tents thrown up along some designated street. Last, but not least, there were the bars. In the community where we moved, Japanese ran the vegetable and dry goods stores; but the bar was run by our new neighbors, a Syrian family, which had recently come to Brazil. Whether we wanted to or not, if we bought milk for our three babies, we had to buy it at the local bar since that was the only place which had refrigeration. A bar in Brazil is not like the closed dark bars in the States. They have wide roll up metal doors that open to the ceiling and leave the bar wide open and well illuminated. They usually sell lunches, soft drinks and a few groceries as well.

OUR FIRST NEIGHBORS

Like all other shop owners, our Syrian neighbors, Senhor George's family had their living quarters in the same building. With just a low fence between our very close houses, we had some interesting times. Neither of our families could carry on a conversation in a common language at first but as time progressed we began to understand one another. Their oldest daughter, Linda, who had come to Brazil with her father before the rest of the family to help set up their business, had a working knowledge of Portuguese. Perhaps her curiosity about us or maybe her natural friendliness caused her to want to talk with us. On our side of the fence, curiosity was just as great. We learned they were not Muslims but Catholics of the Maronite order which is prevalent in that part of the world, especially Lebanon.

Senhor George tried to give Steve a gun so he could help keep robbers away from his bar and our houses if needed. It was true that we lived only a few blocks from an area famous for being the place where many thieves of São Paulo lived but that did not merit Steve accepting the gun.

One of Brazil's greatest explorers and the first director of the Indian Protection Service, Cândido Rondon, when referring to wild tribes, made one of the noblest statements I have ever heard: "Die if necessary; kill, never."

Any missionary going into a dangerous area should certainly have no less a noble attitude than this great man who did not profess to be a born again Christian. We, like all sane missionaries, did not deliberately put ourselves into harm's way; but, if perchance we found ourselves there, then we had to rely heavily on the sovereignty of God. We knew that if it were His will, He was plenty big enough to take care of us, physically and otherwise. May I add now fifty years later, that He never once failed us although the danger had been there all the time.

One day a blood curdling scream came from next door. Neighbors up and down the street poured out of their houses and ran down the street in the direction of an empty lot. Then I saw and heard Linda's mother, doubled up with pain, praying in a heart-wrenching wail in Arabic, head that way. As she ran, she repeatedly raised her hands to heaven and then doubled her body almost as if she were touching the ground. Her son, Little George, had gone out to fly a kite about a block away where someone had carelessly left a wide hand dug well uncovered on the open lot. Little George wasn't paying any attention when he backed up to give more string to his kite as it lifted in the wind and he fell in. He must have fallen a good twelve meters (roughly 39 ft.) before landing on the dry bottom, unhurt! Refusing to trust anyone but himself, Papa George grabbed a long rope from his store, tied it around a pole on one end and lowered it into the well. When he knew that little George had mounted the pole, he pulled him out all by himself, refusing help from other men who had gathered around. All the time he was pulling, he was talking non-stop in Arabic. Poor Papa George was so relieved his son wasn't hurt until when he finally pulled him out, he gave the kid a big swat on the seat of his pants and sent him home in a hurry.

I thought, "What a funny thing to do," until about two years later when I saw my own three year old son along with a neighbor child take turns at swinging between the windlass and the opening of our wide, hand dug well. Not daring to yell at them for fear they might fall, I ran and caught the children before they could do it again. Believe me; I knew exactly how Senhor George felt. Emotions high from fear of what had passed and afraid the child might try it again, I gave my son the spanking of his life. I sent the neighbor kid home in haste so I wouldn't be tempted to do likewise to him. There was nothing funny anymore, when it was my turn, about spanking a kid who had just about stopped your heart from beating. It was far better for the child to remember the scorched pants and not do it anymore than to fall to his death.

Curious to know what Senhor George was saying in Arabic when he pulled his son from the well, Steve later asked him about it.

"Oh, I was praying to Saint George," he answered.

Just to see what his response would be, Steve asked, "Who is Saint George?"

"You know. Same as Jesus Christ," he replied in his broken Portuguese.

"No, Senhor George. You really think your saint is greater than Jesus because, when we are in trouble, we always pray to the one who is the greatest, to our God."

Of course, Steve already knew that St. George had been taken off the official list of saints as being fictitious, but Senhor George didn't know it. Today many would say that what happened was a true miracle performed by St. George. My opinion is that it just wasn't little George's time to go. Who knows what softened his landing in the bottom of the well? Anyway, little George is now a grown man and none the worst for his fall, but not because of father's fictitious saint.

If little George ever became a true believer in Christ or not, I don't know; his sister Linda did. She gives Steve the credit for being the first to evangelize her, although she joined another church and not ours. When she was grown, she married a neighbor boy with whom she had two or three children. Though he was still a young man, he had a serious heart condition, which required open heart surgery. Unfortunately, after returning home, he fell in the bathroom, tearing open the surgery and died. I was told that at his wake, she took off her shoe (this must be an Eastern custom) and beat it on the wall as she cried out, "Why did you up and die on me?"

When we got ready to move, Senhor George came over to tell us how sorry he was that we were leaving. "We hate to see you go," he said, "because you are the first neighbors we have had with whom we have never had a fight!"

Our other neighbors in Cidade Leonor were of varied races, too. We lived in a real "Babylon." The neighbors on the other side of us were from Estonia. They were a little more well to do than the rest of us and very nice. Their son Walter spoke English well enough to translate for the doctor and us when I nearly died with hepatitis.

Three months after we arrived in Brazil, Steve arranged for all of us to go with him to Tupã, a city where many Japanese had settled, to see if the Lord wanted us to work there. On the way there both David and I became extremely ill. The trip took a total of 8 hours on two different trains with the first one being relatively comfortable but when we got on the second one which the Brazilians called "Smoking Mary," a train powered by burning wood, I could hardly sit up. With no comfort at all on the wooden slats of the straight upright benches, our headaches became almost unbearable. By the time we got to the hotel, we both were vomiting. On the fourth day, Steve sent for a Japanese doctor so I could explain my condition. It wouldn't have made any difference if he could only speak Swahili because with me begging him in Japanese to check my liver, he dismissed my pleas as ignorance and insisted that I only had a sore throat. That night I felt I was dying. My hands and feet began to tingle. That's when I turned to the wall and prayed to God that if it were His will, to let me live and raise my babies. He heard my prayer. I went into the deepest sleep I have ever known but woke up the next day with my fever gone. Even though I was a long way from being well, the tide had changed. I knew I had hepatitis and was in a

These My People

bad shape. In a few days we returned to São Paulo the same way we had gone. Some wonderful well-to-do gentleman saw my condition and insisted that we take his Pullman sleeper. No doubt it saved my life. God was still taking care of me.

Back home Steve asked Walter to find a Brazilian doctor who made house calls. When the doctor examined me, he turned to Walter and said, "God is with this woman. I can't find her liver."

All plans to move changed as I had to stay in bed for 3 months and so did our attitude change about working only with the Japanese. That's when Steve started devoting more time to learning the Portuguese language. He met a young Brazilian, Edison, who began tormenting him to teach him English. Steve decided to exchange English for Portuguese if they would use the Bible as the textbook. Before long we had a Bible study going and Steve's knowledge of the language grew. Others began to come to the studies and Steve got out among the people more. As a result, not only Edison received the Lord as Savior but so did Pedro Shigeyoshi, a Japanese man, who lived in another part of town. Steve first heard of this man from a young man who worked in the drug store where we bought medicine. He told Steve how his uncle was searching the Bible to find the truth and asked him to go visit his uncle in Jardim Joá on the south side of São Paulo. Steve made many visits to this man's house to explain the Gospel, which resulted in his salvation. A date was set for Edison and Pedro to be baptized. Steve and I and our three young children went with them to the Interlagos Lake for the first baptism since we had arrived. This meant the beginning of a church and we would not leave São Paulo now.

A missionary does not know by just looking at a person if he or she will receive the gospel therefore many times God's servant is in a vulnerable position among undesirable persons. When Steve had to go to the drug store in Jabaquara, he met several Japanese people. A few of these later received the Lord but one of them brought me nothing but fear and concern. There were times, if I left my front door open, this guy would just walk in and sit down whether I invited him or not. Steve witnessed to this man on every occasion but apparently he didn't believe that we were true missionaries. He told one young man who frequented our meetings that no American would come to Brazil just to preach the gospel; there had to be another reason. When he showed up one day with a couple of strange men who wanted to sell contraband items to us, we had had enough. We decided that when he walked in the door from then on, we would drop everything we were doing, sit down, and read the Bible together and pray. I was so concerned I literally "watched" while Steve prayed. I felt that he might try to kidnap David in an attempt to make us do what he wanted. He had shown an unusual interest in David for some reason. Our defense has always been God and the power of His Word. If perchance our opinion of the man were wrong and if God were truly dealing with him, then he would receive the Word but if not, he would leave us alone. After a few times of this treatment, he stopped coming and our consciences were clear.

Close to the end of our first year in Brazil, the Don Ross family joined us on the mission field and we felt we should organize the church. The fledgling church had its official beginning on December.7, 1958 with four missionaries and the two new Brazilian converts. The Eldwyn Rogers family arrived and joined us in January. I believe with all my heart that the progress of our work, not discounting that it was the Lord who did the work, was due in part to the fact that we three families joined in with these people and became a part of them. The locals know when the missionary puts a wall of separation between himself and them and they are never really very comfortable if he has a superior attitude. I have heard too many locals talk down through the years not to know this.

Even with the many mistakes we all made as green-horn missionaries, there were also a lot of things we did right. One of them was sticking to the Bible way of doing mission work, which always gets biblical results. "Not that we are sufficient of ourselves to think any thing as of ourselves but our sufficiency is of God." 2 Corinthians 3:5. With three families working together, the work grew, not by leaps and bounds but steadily.

MRS. DINAH

One of the new members told us of an elderly South African lady of English origin, who lived nearby. Curious to learn why she came to Brazil, Bro. Rogers and Steve paid her a visit. This is her intriguing story of perseverance and faith.

Mrs. Dinah was raised in a godly, Baptist home in Pretoria, South Africa and received the Lord as her savior at an early age. Given a wonderful education she became the church organist and was active in church work. A young doctor, who became interested in her, began to woo her by pretending to be a Christian, even to the point of joining the church. She never dreamed of what lay ahead of her when she married this doctor or how deceitful he was. Soon after the wedding, they made plans to go to Argentina to set up his practice for he was told he could make a fortune there. It was not long after arriving there that he showed his real character. He told Dinah that the religious façade was over and that there would be no more church or God in their newly formed family. It became increasingly hard for her to serve God as his abuse progressively worsened. If he caught her praying, he would beat her. He even put her Bible in the outdoor toilet to use as paper. She never lost faith but prayed for his salvation. For a while their financial situation was good but as time passed it began to deteriorate. It was then he decided to move to Brazil and work there. He was so wicked; he molested one of his own daughters. Mrs. Dinah continued to pray for him to be saved. By now the reader is probably wondering why in the world she didn't leave him. One must remember that she was an old woman when we met her and back at the turn of the 20th century women put up with a lot due to the fact that they were women. A stranger in a foreign land, isolated from family, and without money, she had no one to turn to but God. Her husband lost what fortune he had as well as his mind. She persisted in prayer for God to let him regain his faculties enough to repent before he died. When we met them, they were extremely poor and he had become bedfast which in itself was probably a blessing. Once when Steve went to witness to him, he asked his wife who Steve was. When she told him that Steve was a preacher, he threw a brick at him but didn't have enough strength to toss it very far! He didn't live too much longer after that but shortly before he died, he regained his normal mind and asked God, his wife and family to forgive him of all his sins. After a lifetime of suffering, Mrs. Dinah's prayers were finally heard, even though she also died soon after that. It is wonderful that her husband was finally saved, but what a shame he had wasted his entire life. It doesn't pay for a person to deliberately go against the truth they know.

THE ADORNOS

A few blocks down the hill from us lived several well-knit families who were more like a clan than anything else and their leader was a man named Lazarus. They had moved to São Paulo city from the extreme western side of the state of São Paulo where they had left several other brothers and sisters and their large families. After selling their farms near a little village called Pioneiros, they came to São Paulo with high hopes of having a better life. When they heard that we were having services nearby, they were delighted to come since most of them were professing Christians in a Baptist Church downtown. This increased our crowd considerably.

Bro. Lazarus was a fine man, well versed in the scriptures, but very easily impressed by any display of diplomas. Since he had no more than a fourth grade education, he prided himself in being self educated, even turning his hand at writing poetry now and then. He heard on the radio about a doctrinal correspondence course that gave a diploma upon completion, so he sent for it. After about the fourth or fifth lesson, he began to believe that the Law of Moses was obligatory for Christians to observe today although he believed that salvation comes by grace. But it was terribly hard for him to give up his pork. One day the temptation was so great he gave in and bought a ham for his wife to cook. It was a special occasion and his family made a feast of it without having any qualms because they did not agree with him on this point. Soon after eating the "forbidden" pork, he became deathly ill and had to go to the hospital where he died within a few days. None of the others who had eaten the ham suffered anything.

All of this taught me clearly what Galatians 5:4 means when it says that "whosoever of you are justified by the law are fallen from grace." In most cases the penalty for breaking the law was physical death so if you put yourself under the law as a way of life, you are automatically under its condemnation and curse without mercy or grace. That doesn't mean a person is eternally lost but it means he might have to pay the consequences for his sin in this life. Our Bro. Lazarus certainly did. "As ye have received Christ, so walk ye in Him." Our walk should match our faith. "The just shall live by faith."

THREE SISTERS

In their visitation, the men came in contact with three sisters who were Spiritualist mediums. Until then we had little knowledge of this cult although many religions including some so-called Christians have varying degrees of spiritualism in their practice. Spiritualism was brought into Brazil by African slaves in the early 16th century. Anyone caught practicing it was punished by death, so they learned to hide it within the Catholic Church's own practices. For example, they would secretly put the name of an African deity on the Catholic saint. In church they would honor the saint, but when no one was around to squeal on them to the authorities, they would switch back to their old ways of making contact with their deity. When religious tolerance was finally granted to the non-Catholic religions, Spiritualism came out into the open. Nevertheless, after being mingled with Catholicism for two centuries, it has left its strong influence on the churches and many times goes hand in hand with some of its practices, especially in the northern states of Brazil. Spiritualism can be classified in two main divisions: the "White Table" kind which claims to only work for the good of humanity and the other lower types such as Voodoo, Macumba, and Candoblé which put spells on others along with their other divinations. All of them supposedly consult the spirits of the dead or of angels to receive their messages concerning the future as to what they should do in any given situation. They believe in the old Babylonian doctrine of reincarnation. Each person has his or her favorite spirit "guide" they try to "bring up" to consult in their séances. To do their work they may place spiritual value on precious or semi-precious stones, small seashells, flowers, clothing or any object of a person they wish to affect. These objects help to enhance their contact with their spirit "guide" to make the connections necessary between

These My People

them and the object of their incantations. The "white table" cult uses light colored candles and the lower classes use black, dark purple or red candles in their ceremonies. They all concentrate in unison whether it's with positive or negative thinking as they make a prayer circle, usually holding hands. The sorceress, called "Mother of the Saint," is a medium or witch, and usually puffs rapidly on a cigar until she falls into a trance where she can make contact with the other world and receive the message desired. At this point her voice changes and supposedly it is the spiritual "guide" who is speaking in and through her. She becomes at that time what they call a "horse" since the spirit uses her to come to the seeker. Before they can become bona fide consultants, these mediums have many rituals they must go through, some of which are horrible. The three sisters mentioned above started out when young by playing with the rituals but as they went deeper into the practice, they became afraid of what they were doing because they were no longer in control and knew that they were being possessed by a force they didn't want. The true gospel was a sweet relief to these women when they accepted Jesus as their savior and were delivered from the grip of Satan. When Jesus comes in, there is no room for demons. Incidentally, when this happens, there is no need for all of the ceremony or show seen in some circles today. There is definitely something wrong if a person claims to be a Christian but is demon possessed. Paul said, "If any man have not the Spirit of Christ, he is none of his."

After the other missionaries got a grip on the language, we began to feel we needed to move on and let them handle the church and mission work in São Paulo. At that time Bro. Lazarus' brothers from Pioneiros made a visit to their relatives in São Paulo and begged us to go to Pioneiros to start a church. At one time there were about 80 people who had attended a mission point led by another Baptist group from a town about four hours away. When the pastor of that church succeeded in getting enough money from them to help build an impressive building where he lived, he abandoned the work. They were never organized into a church and after he left them, many moved away and the group was greatly reduced in number. Only Bro. Lazarus' relatives and a few others remained. Not knowing what to do, they came to us for help. The nearest town, Pereira Barreto, was primarily a Japanese colony and this interested us, so after praying we decided it was God's will for us to move out to the interior.

During our two and half years stay in the city of São Paulo, we had to learn so much. Steve acquired a working knowledge of Portuguese and even though I had no formal language training, I began to pick up the language mostly by listening to sermons and singing hymns and associating what I heard with what was being done. Of course, we all made hilarious mistakes but the Brazilians were patient and kind to us.

There were good and also trying times. Death was a common happening around us. One day our little vegetable delivery boy's shoes were found next to his family's well. He had toppled over the wooden rim and drowned. My neighbor's infant son also died. That was the first time I had ever been to a Brazilian wake. When I walked into the living room where the baby lay covered with a diaper over his face to keep the flies off, I felt a terrible foreboding. His mother asked me to remove the diaper so I could see him. When I did, I got a big jolt. I was not expecting to see his eyes wide open. They had not been able to close his eyelids after death.

I was expecting a baby myself. Michael Ray had been born a year and few months earlier, but our fifth child was on the way. Try as I may, I could not remove the sadness which engulfed me. Mark was born a month early and died the next day. Part of me now is one with Brazilian soil.

As soon as I was strong enough, we moved to the far western part of the State of São Paulo, where Pioneiros was located. This village would become such a part of me until even now, nearly 50 years later, every time I hear a rooster crow early in the morning, I feel a tug on my heart for the times we lived among those pioneer people.

We left São Paulo in June of 1960 and would return to São Paulo in 1964, but for the time in between we were in Pioneiros and Pereira Barreto.

CHAPTER SIX
FRONTIER LIFE IN PIONEIROS
1960-1961

Pioneiros (Pioneers) was the right name for the village we moved to in 1960. Its inhabitants were hardy, self sufficient, ingenious people who lived up to their name. Although many had less then a fourth grade education, I learned very quickly not to underestimate their intelligence. A college entrance exam may measure what you have studied; but out on the frontier the true test of your IQ is endurance and survival. Wild animals were still to be contended with in some places. Down by the river, the anacondas crossed the wide swift currents with the ease of a speedboat. *Piranhas* could eat an animal in split seconds, if it fell in the water. The pioneers had become masters in reading the signs of nature and knew how to outwit what lurked in the wild. In this area where burning the woods was a constant thing, we never saw a wild forest fire. I can't remember any fire getting out of control or even going beyond where it was intended to go. Probably, the hardest problem to contend with here was not the big wild things but sicknesses brought on by the tiny world of insects.

If we had arrived in a covered wagon instead of the Volkswagen van we purchased before leaving São Paulo, it would have been more in harmony with the setting. This village was settled a few years prior to our arrival by pioneers who had bought small farms carved out of a huge undeveloped *fazenda* (plantation or ranch) belonging to one owner, who contrary to the usual way of selling large farms as a whole, decided to break up his land to give the smaller farmers a chance to own their own properties. Many of these small farmers were still in the process of clearing the lands and burning the timber to make room for crops and cattle when we arrived on the scene. There were several farms, though, that were well on the way to being developed and productive. Some farmers had coffee trees already producing, but on a whole there was still much untilled land that needed clearing, especially down near the Tietê River. Oxen and horses were used to work their farms as well as being their chief means of transportation. A constant haze of smoke from the burning of pastures and virgin timber hid the mid-day sun. In spite of all the hardship we were about to undergo, we were indeed privileged to experience something similar to what our forefathers had gone through when they cleared away lands in the beginning of our own country. Thank the Lord for my humble beginnings! I would need every skill of survival I had ever learned as a child on our farm to cope with life out here on this frontier of our mission work.

As we began to draw near our destination June 29, 1960 the progressively shrinking roads made me concerned about what would happen if we met an oncoming vehicle. My worry was all in vain because nothing appeared in our path. In fact, I could not tell if there was any kind of life on the other side of the thick tall colonial grass which cascaded down both sides of the road and cut off our view. It made me wonder if my husband had somehow found "the uttermost part of the earth" on which to take our last stand. Steve's mother once admonished him not to go so far he would have to preach only to the monkeys. Maybe she was right after all.

When we finally came to an opening, I could see a little village with one wide red dirt street running through the middle. It looked like there were five or six streets cutting across it to form a few blocks of houses on each side. As was the custom of most interior towns, the Established Church dominated the highest point near the center of the settlement. There were two drug stores of a sort, a couple of general stores, a butcher shop and many more saloons than necessary. It would have provided an excellent set for a good old western movie. To complete the scenery, as we entered the village, I could hear the clop of the cowboys' horses and the metallic sound of their spurs in the stirrups as they jingled about their business. There were many two wheel carts laden with farm produce drawn by oxen. Horses were tied to posts in front of the saloons where their owners were picking up "courage" to encounter their tasks. On the far edge of town was the cattle trail where droves of cattle passed frequently on the way to market in another town.

Steve had told me before we left São Paulo that he had purchased a "nice" house constructed with "material." By that he meant it was not the typical "*pau-a-pique*" house made of palm tree strips daubed with mud and covered overhead by a crude thatched roof. The locals called an adobe type brick, "material." My house was made of these bricks with roofing of red tile slates. I really didn't know what to expect as we drove up to our new home. I just knew that we wouldn't have electricity or running water.

One advantage of never expecting anything special in the way of comfort when a person goes to the mission field is that he is never disappointed with what he finds. When I opened the doors of the house, all I could see were black walls staring me in the face. Instead of screened glass windows, there were only rough wood shutters barring the light. This place looked dismal. I looked up and didn't see a ceiling;

These My People

I looked down and saw that half of the house had red cement floors and the other half had plain adobe brick laid in dirt. In the kitchen over in a corner was the culprit of all the black soot on the walls. Built in with the house my new stove looked like two giant red cement steps made with a three eyed iron plate right down the middle of the top step. The bottom step protruded enough to hold a log or kindling which was slid in the opening under the iron plate. There was absolutely no way for all the smoke to be drawn up, into, and out of the chimney, thus the sooty walls.

I walked out on the back porch, which was really a lean to, and surveyed the rest of our property. I had been told it had a "modern" laundry. Many of the houses had a slab of wood set at a steep angle so the women could take a wet soapy garment from a basin or tub, sling it around in the air for momentum, and pop it down hard on the slab in such a way as to force the dirt out. (They always hoped that the buttons wouldn't go with the dirt.) But my laundry had two cement square tubs with a cement slab in the middle. This was a real luxury. I could pop my buttons on a cement slab instead of a wooden one!

My big hand dug well stood conveniently close to the porch. At first glance, it looked like one of those old quaint romantic wishing wells you see in pictures. I knew from childhood experience that the romance was only in the beholding. When we first got there, it had plenty of water and then when the drought came several months later, this well became my wishing well in truth. I wished everyday it had water! God taught me to say, "Thank you, Father, for water."

Our shower stall over to the side of the porch was a closed in box with walls up just high enough to keep from being immodest as you bathed. The shower itself consisted of a big bucket tied to a rope, which was lowered to fill and was raised to bathe. At the bottom of the bucket a makeshift shower-head was welded on. All of this system was known as "*Tiradentes*" (tooth jerker) in honor of a dentist who was hanged when fighting for Brazil's independence and became a national hero. I thought the name was quiet appropriate for another reason. A body might just loose some teeth while manipulating it if the contraption were not tied down properly.

I can't leave out our outhouse. It was a fairly well made little wooden house on the back of the property. Covered by a tile roof, it had a cement floor for which I became exceedingly grateful later when I heard tales of some neighbors' rickety toilet floors giving way, carrying the occupants with them. The accommodation consisted of only one long narrow slit about 4"x 12" in the floor. That was reason enough to be thankful; the children would not fall through!

We arrived in Pioneiros on Thursday, and early Saturday morning, I already had visitors. Some of the ladies from the farms had come to welcome me. They all brought some gift from their farms: eggs, milk, coffee, and a chicken whose feet were tied together with corn shucks. These were the most precious gifts I could receive since arranging food here would be a daily struggle for me. The village butcher killed a cow two to three times a week and hung the meat up in open air. Because of the lack of refrigeration (and sanitation!) we had to cook and eat it before it spoiled. That's why a live chicken was such a wonderful gift; it could stay fresh until I needed it.

My Portuguese had a lot to be desired at that time. The ladies were very timid so you can imagine how well we conversed. I did hear one little girl exclaim to her mother, "Mama, look how beautiful her house is!"

Inside me, I laughed. Sorry, but I failed to see the beauty. Only when I returned the little girl's visit did I see how really wonderful my house was. Her folk's house was the "*pau-a-pique*" type made with split palm trees tied together with vines, and daubed with mud. I think about half the mud daubing was missing from the walls. The floors were of uneven dirt. We sat on rickety homemade benches.

"Yes, little girl, my house is beautiful. May I always remember that," was my inward thought as I observed everything.

Saturday night the whole village was warned against us. The priest who visited the village turned up the volume to maximum on the loud speaker that was mounted on his old jeep and bellowed out, "Beware, brethren. A foreign wolf has just arrived in our midst. Be careful!" This was repeated several times so that all could get the message. This particular priest really wasn't a bad guy. He was just doing his duty. In fact, in time he became quite friendly with Steve. One day Steve asked him if he really believed in all the idols hanging on his church wall.

Here was his answer: "Of course not. We have those up there because our people are ignorant."

Steve then asked, "Why are your people so ignorant, if there were priests on the first ships to Brazil? You've had 400 years to educate your people."

The friendly friar was not like his elder fellow priest who tried to run us off of the road with a big truck. We were going to the nearest town, Pereira Barreto, in our Volkswagen van with all of our kids. When he saw who we were, he deliberately turned his big cargo truck in our direction. Had not the Lord helped Steve swerve out of his way, my story would be another today. All this happened before Pope John the 23rd changed their church's policy on dealing with non-Catholics. We have read of earlier Baptist missionaries who paid dearly for preaching the gospel in Brazil before religious liberty was granted. Even after it was legally granted, there was still a lot of intolerance.

Soon after we settled in, Steve had to go twelve miles to Pereira Barreto, the county seat, to get his Brazilian driver's license. His temporary driver's permit would soon be out of date and he had a deadline to get the car documents in order. This is why he had to meet our sheriff.

OUR SHERIFF

After many unfruitful trips to see the sheriff, Steve's patience was just about gone. He still had not learned that *amanha* doesn't necessarily mean tomorrow but just means "not now." The sheriff loved to fish and hunt very much so official business was always better "tomorrow." Steve was told several times to "come back tomorrow," and since he urgently needed his driver's license, he kept going back.

Getting up early one morning to get this business over with, Steve arrived before the sheriff came to his office. (Steve was like that. I have never known us to be late for anything.) He was told that the sheriff was not in but would be there later. With time on his hands Steve meandered down the street till he came to the local hotel. Out on the sidewalk a handful of men were idly conversing as they relaxed on a bench. Seeing them, Steve struck up a conversation and spoke in Japanese to the hotel manager whom he had met earlier. The others were surprised and asked, "Where did you learn to speak Japanese so fluently?"

One distinct gentleman in the group who was wearing sunglasses began to ask Steve a lot of questions, which he was more than glad to answer. He wanted to know what brought him to Brazil and to their town. By this time Steve was primed to vent his feelings about never finding the sheriff in town. "What kind of sheriff do you folks have here? He is always gone fishing or hunting. When does he ever do his work? A criminal could come in and rob a bank and never be caught!"

At this point the fellow with the sunglasses agreed with Steve and also added a few grievances of his own. This encouraged Steve to comment even more about the absentee sheriff. Some time later, Steve went back to the police station to see if the sheriff were in or not.

When he went in, the secretary told him to have a seat and wait a few minutes. In a little while he was ushered into the sheriff's office. There sat the fellow with the sun glasses who had asked most of the questions out on the street! He said, "Hello, reverend. We meet again!" Believe it or not, the driver's license was granted that day and this was the beginning of a real friendship between the two. He also allowed Steve freedom to speak to the prisoners in jail at any time.

We learned to really respect this sheriff. When he closed down the city's red light district, he made several very angry enemies. One day in a vegetable store, a certain man who had lost money with the closing down of the district, walked in and shot him. The bullet missed the sheriff's heart and lungs but did lodge in his arm. He calmly walked across the street to Dr. Alexander's office and said, "Dig it out, Doc."

Sunday services were begun at noon instead of in the morning. It seemed odd to us *norteamericanos* to begin church at noon. We had always observed the American custom of Sunday morning worship. Out here American religious customs meant nothing because all these folk had to do their farm chores before going to church. Nearly all of them had been up well before dawn to milk their cattle and get their milk out to the road to be picked up by a truck from the local cheese factory. If a person has never had a cow to worry with, this may sound like he is putting his work before the Lord, but it isn't. The brethren had more time to worship if they put all their chores behind them first. Many walked about seven miles on dirt roads to come to church and then return home after church. At night these roads might have unseen poisonous snakes curled up in their paths. Brave people that they were, our brethren came regardless of that danger. I loved their dedication.

Moving to Pioneiros, we were totally immersed into Brazilian culture. We were the only North Americans in the area and all of our contacts were with the Brazilians themselves. Steve was invited to officiate at a wedding a couple of weeks after we arrived but he declined the offer because he could not legally marry them. They didn't seem to understand and frankly we didn't either. Until religious liberty [actually toleration] was granted around the turn of the 19th century, all marriages and births were only legal if registered in the Catholic Church. The government took control of all legal documents, and marriage had to be performed by the judge or justice of the peace. Priests and preachers could perform the religious ceremony, but the marriage was only valid if the civil ceremony was performed. This resulted in two ceremonies; one by the civil authorities and another by the minister chosen by the participants. We were not aware of all this.

Weddings in Brazil are expensive. I have never been to one, be it ever so humble, that would not put American weddings to shame for the amount of food served. At that first wedding, we learned that the bride's parents had killed two steers, several pigs, and who knows how many chickens! Beside all this meat, there were large tubs full of other food. Most Brazilians had a deathly fear of drinking anything cold so our soft drinks were at room temperature.

"Weddings in the green church," as they were called, were very common. The couple would elope without the benefit of a civil or religious ceremony. Usually their parents didn't mind since it took away any obligation to throw an expensive reception. By the time of our arrival, there were many couples that just lived together instead of going thru the expense of two weddings.

These My People

Some of these men refused to legalize their marriages. Many left their families to root for themselves while they moved somewhere else where they arranged other families. If they were not married in the church, their consciences would not bother them, since they were still considered "single." If they were not married in civil court, they had no legal responsibility to their families which made it convenient to start another family. There were plenty of men who had several families at the same time. Infidelity was expected among men but not tolerated in the women. This kind of situation caused many fights resulting in death of one partner or the other. For example, just before we moved there, a big rancher had an "*amante*" (lover) with whom he preferred to live instead of his wife. Since divorce was illegal at that time, he killed his pregnant wife and threw her in their well. He was arrested and thrown in jail, but for only a short period of time. After getting out, he married his lover, and got all his money and property. Supposedly, he was converted in jail and decided to become a minister of some off brand religion. Murder in Brazil did not carry a harsh sentence so he could have his cake and eat it too.

I heard of another case where a poor longsuffering woman had had enough of her drunken, no-good man. She waited for him to get really drunk one day, treated him kindly and put him to bed, then buried a hatchet in his head when he was sound asleep. That took care of that problem.

Sickness was an ever-present concern. That part of the country was well known as the most infested with the barber bug (Trypanosoma cruzi), which caused the Chagas disease. The bug came out at night to suck blood from a person, usually around the face and neck area, thus the name. When he finished, he would then defecate on the spot where he had sucked. The virus entered the body by means of the puncture. We had people die in our car on the way to the hospital because of this dreaded disease. An untold number of our acquaintances either died or had a lifelong struggle with it. The parasite usually attacked a nerve controlling the heart muscles or some other vital organ. If it went to the main nerves, the person lived about two weeks, but if it went to a less vital area, they could live longer but would always be bothered by its effect. Just before we moved out to Pioneiros, the government set up an insect control system. Everyone was obligated to let them spray their houses inside and out with DDT. The walls looked as if they had been whitewashed with the spray. The poison was so strong, it killed the rats as well as the bugs. As far as I know, none of my family contracted the Chagas disease while we lived there and the excessive use of insecticide apparently did no harm. All I can say is that the Lord looked over us because the danger was all around us.

Everybody had a long list of homemade remedies for just about any ailment. Perhaps of all the people in the village, I was the only one at that time who had any instruction about diseases, which was pitifully small in face of all the sicknesses. It made no difference anyway. Since I was still young and a foreigner to boot, "Grandma Maria's" teas were the tried and proven way for treating diseases, and any advice I might give was not to be trusted. If a concoction Grandma made wouldn't work, then the "Mãe de Santo" (witch, sorceress or medium) could be called in to work a miracle.

The country people had a saying they liked to repeat when someone gave them a remedy for a sickness. It went something like this, "*pinga com que?*" (sugar cane liquor with what?") In other words, liquor was almost always used with some herb they had planted in their yard. No doubt some of these herbs really had medicinal value. I saw many foxglove plants in yards and warned people to be careful about making tea with it. They had no idea what it was, much less know it contained digitalis, but somebody's grandma said that it was good for your heart.

Another type of treating sickness was *"simpatia,"* or "sympathetic magic." It worked this way: if a person had an earache, he would take three cow hooves and heat them by the open fire. He would bury one of them, throw one over his shoulder, and then lay the third one on his ear to remove the earache. Using the last one, which was warm, made sense to me since putting something warm over a painful area might ease it, but why the other two? There were untold numbers of remedies like this. At that time doctors were few and far between so the common person had to rely on his own resources which were not always scientific.

Besides our van, there was only one other car in the village, the local taxi service. When its owner was not available, people naturally came to Steve to get him to take them wherever they wanted to go. All Steve ever asked of them was to pay for the gas. If the taxi were available, he would refer them to him. We never knew what to expect when someone asked us to take them places. Steve's Volkswagen Kombi became the village ambulance service.

One day a father and his two sons were building a store near us, when the old man made a false move and fell off the roof. His sons came running to Steve to take their unconscious dad to the hospital in Pereira Barreto. Just before they arrived at the hospital, the old man regained consciousness and seemed to be all right. When they returned home, the boys didn't want to pay for the gas because the old man had lived! I guess, if he had died, they would have felt obligated to pay.

On another occasion, a peon of one of our church members staggered up to our house and asked Steve to take him to the drug store as fast as possible. Steve put him in the van and stopped at the drug store, which was like a first aid station in our village. When the owner saw the problem, he told Steve to rush the man to a hospital immediately. He would not touch the man. Back in the van, the peon begged Steve to go faster. Glancing back at the fellow, Steve saw blood pouring out of the guy's boot. He grabbed a role of toilet paper we always carried in the van and threw it to him.

"I don't know where you are hurt, but for goodness sake, press this to the bleeding area," Steve hollered to him as the van bounced around on the rough road.

In desperation the peon cried, "Just go faster."

When they got to the hospital in Pereira Barreto, not one of the town's three doctors was there. The nurse refused to admit him. That's when Steve came unglued. He said, "Oh yes, you are going to admit him. I got him here alive and now you are going to take care of him."

When she saw how excited Steve was, she decided to look for herself and that was enough. She got in touch with the doctor immediately. After examining him, the doctor called the police and told Steve that he could not leave but would have to be a witness to the emergency operation. The doctor refused to touch the man without legal protection. The man had basically castrated himself in an attempt to lance an infected area that he had injured by falling from his horse on a small jagged stump a few days earlier. The doctor didn't know that Steve couldn't tolerate the sight of blood very well. In the operating room Steve backed up against the wall for support and tried to stand the situation. In a little while the doctor glanced over at Steve, who by then was turning green and was ready to slide down the wall. "Reverend, get out of here," he shouted. Steve barely made it out in time to keep from fainting. The guy's life was spared, but he would always be a eunuch from then on.

Once a young couple came to get Steve to carry them to the next town so they could elope. Steve refused them.

Every kid in the village wanted to ride in our van, but our boys wanted to ride their horses. If you opened the doors of the car, any number of the kids would pile in. Many times I heard the expression, "This car has the heart of a mother. It will always hold one more." They meant that no matter how full the car was, they fully intended to go with us!

Traveling on the dirt roads was always an experience. The hoe, shovel, and tow sack were all standard equipment we had to carry to get us out of sand or mud when we got stuck. We learned this after a few mishaps.

At any given time on the dirt roads we might run into a cattle drive. Our kids loved this. If the van were headed into them face on, the cattle would part very nicely to each side of the car. The car would get jostled around some by the cattle rubbing its sides but it wasn't a big hassle. We would have to go very slowly just in case some stubborn steer or cow refused to budge. There were times their heads were jammed up against the window and I wondered if I were going to have a cow jump into my lap, but, fortunately, that never happened. Coming up behind them was different. The cowboys would have to lead the way with their whip as they parted the cattle for us to move through them. We had to stay right behind the horse or the cattle would crowd in between us and the cowboy. Our car became just another moving object in a sea of Brahmas. Many times it was necessary to roll down the window and hit a cow on her rump or yell at her. It was not unusual to go through cattle drives with as many as fifteen hundred head.

Back at the house we always knew when a cattle drive was on the way. Since we lived only a couple of blocks from their trail, we could hear the jingle of the cook's mules laden with pots and pans hours before the herd came along. He had to go ahead and set up camp to have a hot meal waiting for the cowboys.

Jeannie Montgomery

When a cow would get loose from the drove, children and grownups alike ran into whatever house was nearby without asking anyone's permission. Everyone was afraid of these half wild cattle.

Another problem was the climate. If you have ever seen a rain in Louisiana, just double the heaviest and then imagine what a downpour is like in Brazil. After one such rain that lasted only two hours, I ventured out to see what happened nearby. A couple of blocks from our house, the road was gone and in its place was a gully big enough to completely hold an eighteen wheeler. Immediately, I thought of what forty days and nights could do with a rain like that. Yes, I believe in Noah's flood!

Brazil is a land of contrasts. In the rainy season you feel like building an ark; in the hot dry season, you look for water. When we had a drought in 1961 before city water came into use, most of the wells went dry including ours. Jealous owners of the few deeper wells watched carefully over them. All of us were at the mercy of these well owners. My neighbor had a well that didn't dry up; but when he got tired of people always drawing his water, he announced that his dog had climbed upon the well and vomited in it. I doubted his story.

HELP OUT OF THE NIGHT

Between our town and the big city where Steve had to go to have a tooth extracted there is a stretch of rough dirt road about sixty miles long. While he was getting his tooth taken care of, bad weather came up and made the road perilous. It took the dentist over an hour to pull his tooth and by the time he finished, Steve's face was considerably swollen. He was miserable but had to make an attempt to get home. When he left, it was nighttime and raining. He did right well until about 12-15 miles from Pioneiros, where the road became impassable.

These My People

Going up a steep upgrade the car slid into the ditch. Being by himself in the rain, Steve resigned himself to spending the cold night stuck in the mud but asked the Lord to help. It was cold and he had no coat or blanket to wrap up in.

Out of the pitch black night a voice said, "Mister, do you need help?"

Those were sweet words to a sick helpless man. When Steve turned on his lights, he saw a farm hand standing there who told him he would go get a hoe. Suddenly he was gone in the dark, but shortly appeared with a hoe in his hand. He started scraping a path for the wheels so Steve could get the car back on the road. When he did, the man told Steve that he would go with him a little farther on because there was another place he would probably get stuck. And a few miles up the road, he got out and again cleared the road so Steve could pass. This time he told Steve he thought he could make it to the village but gave him his hoe just in case he might need it. The man walked back to his home in the rain. Steve managed to get home even though he was in pain from his swollen jaw which had pieces of the broken tooth the dentist had failed to get out. Even so we rejoiced in how the Lord had sent help out of the night. It's good to be in God's hands.

Steve waited a few days until the weather and his jaw were better to return the hoe. He carried a Bible to give the family. The man had never seen one before but said he had heard about it. Only his young son could read. Steve asked him to read to the family every day. Later Steve returned to visit the family but they had moved away. Like so many farm hands, they were always going from one farm to another to get work. At least these carried God's Word with them to the next place.

JOAQUIN AND JOSEFA

Only God knows what we owe this beloved couple. From the start they treated us like their own. The Lord promised that if we give up brothers, sisters, fathers, and mothers for his name's sake he will give us an hundred fold. We could not have a blood relative treat us any better.

I remember the first morning we arrived in Pioneiros. It was a cold windy day with dust blowing everywhere. Josefa asked us to come eat breakfast with her. We were glad to put our feet under her table because everything was closed in the village because of a holiday, and we had nothing to eat. None of us minded the chickens and pigs running between our legs under the table or the dust that was flying in the air. Ducks waddling around and dogs waiting expectantly near the table for a morsel of food did not ruin our appetites. We blended in with the scenery and enjoyed every bit of it.

On one side of Joaquin's farm lived his brother Mario and family; on the other were his sister, Lola and family. These three families made up the backbone of our church. They became our family. Over the years we were with them in the birth of their children, in their conversion and baptism, marriage and also at their funerals. Their joys were ours, and we shared their tears.

MARIO AND MARIA

Mario was not as energetic as his brother but did have quite a number of cattle on his farm. He, like his brother, was very faithful in the church until the day he died. The rest of Mario and Maria's story will appear later.

LOLA AND FAMILY

Lola's husband had died before we met her. Evidently he was a successful farmer since he left them fairly well fixed in life. Their story also will appear in a later chapter to maintain a chronological order.

Brazilians have a very special sense of humor. There were times when our church men went on horseback to remote places to carry the Gospel. On one such occasion Bro. Joaquin saddled up two of his horses, one for him and one for Steve. One was very nervous and hard to control; the other very slow and gentle. They looked very much alike. Once before, Steve rode the gentle one and thought he was going to ride it again so he asked for spurs. Joaquin, seeing that he had mounted the feisty one, decided to have a little fun with the preacher. Steve spurred the horse which almost shot out from under him. He was on the wrong horse! All the peons in the yard keeled over laughing at the gringo. After calming down some, and starting on their way to make their visit, Joaquin laughed and said, "Bro. Steve, that horse is very intelligent; all I have to say to that horse is...," then raising his voice, he finished his sentence with a loud "GO." The horse once more shot off like a bullet with Steve hanging on for dear life.

Another example of their humor was when we were going to São Paulo on a visit and made a rest stop at a dinky little gas station. They served hot coffee so Steve decided to have a cup. When he started to drink, he saw a roach leg floating around in his cup.

"Sir, there's a roach's leg in my coffee," he informed the owner.

Without cracking a smile the owner replied, "Oh, no, Sir. It's not in your coffee."

"But look at it," Steve insisted as he pulled the leg up with his spoon. "This is a roach leg."

Jeannie Montgomery

The owner said: "Sir that roach leg was not in your coffee. It was in the sugar!"

A NEW BABY

We had been in Pioneiros several months when George, a new member of our church, announced the birth of his son. Steve went out to his farm to visit the new baby's proud parents. During the conversation George said that he wanted to give his baby a Bible name, but it had been difficult to choose from so many. He finally settled on two names. He decided to call him David.

Out of curiosity Steve asked, "And what was the other Bible name you almost picked?"

"Leviticus," he replied.

Trying to keep a straight face, Steve said, "Brother, you made a wise choice."

OUR CHURCH PEOPLE

While the church grew, our love for this people also increased. They shared what they had with us. It was not easy for someone who was not a farmer to find food everyday. We were given milk every morning as long as we were there. When they harvested their rice and beans, we were given enough for our family. Of course, we had to learn to eat the same things they did, but that wasn't hard for a girl raised in Louisiana where rice and beans are common everyday food. Besides that, Brazilian country cooking is very good.

I learned a lot from these people. Without electricity or running water, they managed wonderfully. If they butchered a pig or cow, they smoked what sausage they made and sun-dried the rest. They had a way of cutting a chunk of meat so it would unroll to be an inch thick and

These My People

about a yard long. After letting it soak in briny water over night, they would then throw it across the clothes line in the heat of the day to dry out. A few days of this treatment was enough to preserve it. It could then be rolled up and stored for later use.

They never threw away anything. Tomato sauce cans and cooking oil cans were used to make cups and dippers. (I still catch myself looking at the cans I open here in the States to size them up for future use.) Any bottle was carefully saved and could be used to put pepper sauce in or if it were large enough, it could hold milk. Since corks were not common, corn shucks were twisted and wadded to make stoppers. Corn shucks were wonderful. I have seen them used for everything from making a mattress to tying a door shut on an old truck.

Nearly all of the country folk were very hospitable. Once an elderly couple insisted that we make them a visit out on their little newly cleared place down by the river. We knew they were poor but decided it was best to go have coffee with them. As was my custom, I headed for the kitchen where the women folk were busy while Steve talked to the men. I overheard the lady send her daughter to the neighbors to borrow some coffee cups since she didn't have any. When she returned with them, the lady of the house felt she needed to wash the cups before serving us. My stomach did a flip-flop. She took her finger with which she had just cleaned out her sore eyes and started running it around the inside of the cups to clean them with plain cold water. I knew that Steve and I had to drink that coffee and not offend anyone, but I did try to stop my children from drinking it. It was true that I didn't let them drink coffee at night so that is what I told the lady of the house. If my kids had not been so outgoing, I could have protected them, but instead of being quiet they all yelled, "Yes, we drink coffee." That made me look like a liar, so we all ended up drinking coffee. God took care of us anyway, not because my faith was so great, but because he had mercy; and no one got sick.

Just before Steve went out to Pioneiros the first time, something happened which everybody liked to talk about. One of Lola's young girls went out in the pasture to bring home the cows. She looked up in a tree and saw a big cat. Scared, she ran to her Uncle Joaquin's house, which was nearby, to tell him about it. He and a couple of his peons went to see what was going on. Sure enough, there was a mighty big cat, a jaguar, perched in the tree. They had brought along an old muzzle loader gun that had to have gunpowder, wadding and buckshot stuffed into it to shoot. Since the first shot didn't phase the jaguar because the powder was too weak, they made a very risky decision. Two of the men stood under the tree to keep the jaguar from coming down while the others went back to the house for more powder and shot. This they did and then loaded the gun with a triple load. Amazingly, the gun didn't blow up in their faces and they hit the "cat." On the way down the jaguar caught hold of a four inch diameter limb with its mouth and ripped it off the tree as if it were a twig. When it hit the ground, it died, fortunately. The men then carried it home where the women folk rendered out jaguar oil. It was considered a good medicine for arthritis and a number of other things.

We soon moved to the village and organized the church with eighteen members. Out in the interior it was the custom for men to sit on one side of the church building and the women on the other. Children were almost always made to sit with their mother. If perchance a young couple were courting, they would still sit on opposite sides.

JOÃO AND IRACEMA

Before long we began to notice one of Lola's sons, João, and a young lady, Iracema, come in the church about the same time in every service. Naturally, they obeyed the unwritten rule of where to sit. What I thought was very funny was that after church when he walked her home, they still maintained their distance. He walked on one side of the road and she on the other. We never guessed that they were engaged until one Saturday morning João invited us to their wedding. Thinking that the date would be a few weeks away, Steve asked him when did he intend to marry.

Without wasting words he replied, "Ten o'clock."

It was almost that time then. Steve hurriedly dressed for the occasion and went. The rest of us didn't have time. These country people didn't waste time on frivolities, but they did want to be sure all was legal and had God's approval. I didn't know at the time what a bond I would come to have with them.

Years later Iracema told me about herself. She was a heavy drinker when she accepted the Lord. It was a struggle to give it up, but God gave her grace. She worked very hard out in the fields as a common day laborer and her feet would crack with the red dirt getting in the cracks. The day before she was to be married, she gave herself a pedicure by soaking her feet in a Clorox solution. She and I have shared many laughs and tears.

The year and half we stayed in Pioneiros was long enough to make us one with our people there. We moved to the next town, Pereira Barreto, to start another church, but we never completely left them. Later, after working in yet another town, we returned to the area and labored several years among them.

CHAPTER SEVEN
Pereira Barreto
1961-1963

Pereira Barreto, founded by Japanese immigrants long before World War II when Brazil opened her doors to large number of foreigners, was only about twelve miles from Pioneiros. It was originally called "New Orient." The Japanese language was heard as frequently on the streets as Portuguese. When a couple from the Pioneiros Church moved there, we began to pray about starting a new church there also. With the arrival of Bro. Aderbal and his family from Sao Paulo to help in the work, we were free to go.

Our first house in Pereira Barreto only had four little rooms with a kitchen separate and apart from the main house. It was very much like many other houses in town. For the first time since moving to the interior, we had the luxury of electricity at night even though it was weak and precarious.

The drought in the whole area was severe. The religious leaders of the town told the people that the lack of rain was caused from too many *"crentes"* (believers) coming to town. Men cursed God and all who didn't believe as they did. In spite of all that was being said, the mercy of God was great. (He sends the rain on the just and unjust alike.) He soon sent us a rain, and what a rain! It was a thunderstorm. I saw the tiles on our roof flop up and down as the wind blew. I felt the spray of rain coming through them on my face as I wondered how long the roof would hold out. It was very frightening, but shortly before night, the rain eased up. Stepping down into my outside kitchen, I could hardly see. As I reached up to turn on the light dangling from the rafters, I felt something curl around my leg. Screaming I jumped straight up and felt it fall off. Steve heard me and came running. When he saw I wasn't hurt, he and our neighbor looked around the yard to find the culprit. My chill bumps had chill bumps when I saw it was one of Brazil's most deadly snakes. Isn't it wonderful we serve a God who owns the whole animal kingdom and they can't harm us unless He permits them to do so?

We lived in that house only a short time before we moved to the center of town. One of our members had made some kind of deal with the owner of a *fazenda* [farm or ranch]. A large house in town was part of the deal, and we were able to buy it at a good price. Of all of the houses I have lived in, this was my favorite. There was room enough to spare.

"When goods increase, they are increased that eat them..." (Ecclesiastes 5:11) God didn't give us a big house without a reason.

ABIMAEL

One night a young man slipped onto the back bench where our church service was already in progress. We were using an ex-bar we had rented. When we heard a new voice join in with ours during the singing, we knew he was a believer. He told us that he had just come into town when he heard us singing "At The Cross," and he knew he had found "his people."

Back in Bahia, a northern state of Brazil, he had been engaged to a girl who was not a believer. Later he began to understand that a believer should not marry someone who is not of the same faith, so he began to pray for God to make his fiancé break their engagement. God heard his prayer, and she broke it off without any provocation on his part. In that part of the country it was a terrible shame to break an engagement, and sometimes the family would even shoot the young man who did it. In short, he was scared stiff; so he fled town in a hurry. He hitched a ride in the back of a big truck used to haul immigrants from Bahia to Sao Paulo where big farm owners would hire them as farm hands. This trip took about three or four days. Somehow he found work on the back side of our state not too far from where we lived. At the farm where he was sent, he fell into a forced labor trap. At that time the layout of the farms was very much like our old plantation system with a big house surrounded by the smaller houses where the farm hands lived. The farm had its own little chapel and store where the workers bought their supplies. Although there were some good owners, others used this to keep their help in bondage. They were never given enough money to pay for everything and had to put their purchases on credit at the farm's own store. That way the workers would always be in debt to the owner. The only way to go anywhere was by a vehicle owned by the farm. Once they were there, it was dangerous to attempt to leave. There were watch dogs everywhere. The administrator and owner were the law and order of the land, and woe to the person who tried to run away. Many runaways simply disappeared without a trace left behind.

It didn't take Abimael long to realize that he had really gotten himself into a terrible situation. One day when he was once again nearly bitten by a rattlesnake out in the fields, he turned his face to heaven and prayed, "Lord, I can't keep on living this way. I need my people; help me find them. Please help me escape."

These My People

He carefully devised a plan that he immediately put into effect. He purposed in his heart to walk at night until he came to a main thoroughfare. Also he asked God to send him a ride that would take him to the town where he could find some of "his people." Wherever the driver was going Abimael would accept that as being God's will for him. With all this in mind he managed to escape the barking dogs and to get away undetected at night. He walked to the main dirt road before dawn. Soon the farm trucks started coming by, and he caught a ride with one. As soon as it stopped, Abimael asked the driver, before he could ask him the same question, "Where are you going?"

The driver replied, "Pereira Barreto."

"Well, that's where I'm going, too. Would you give me a lift?"

When they got into town, the driver left him at that little room and board place within earshot of our church. He had hardly arrived, when he heard us singing a few doors down the street from him. With fear that we might dismiss before he got there, he left everything and ran to where we were, following the sound of the music. After church we took him home with us.

Just one look at his meager clothing told us he was in need of help. Steve asked him to stay with us until he found better arrangements, which he did. Steve helped him find work at a shop where they make the wooden parts of truck beds. In time he became their best worker. As he progressed in skill and finances, he gradually worked his way back up north. Today he and his sons are doing quite well as owners of a nice cabinet shop in Rondonia.

MY WIFE'S A WOODPECKER

On one of our many house visits, we met an interesting elderly couple. The lady of the house was an Episcopalian. Her husband tried his best to pronounce that in Portuguese but could only say woodpecker and never could get it right. He would say, "My wife's a *peek-a-pau*," (a woodpecker).

"But, sir, your wife can't be a *peek-a-pau*," Steve insisted.

"Oh yes, she is. She goes down there to that *peek-a-pau* Church where the pastor is Japanese," he kept saying. It then dawned on us that he meant the Episcopal Church. The old man was not making fun of her religion; he just couldn't pronounce it right, especially when he had a few drinks!

MY RED HEADED BABY

Our last child, Steven, was born with red hair. Most people in Pereira Barreto had never seen a redheaded person. Shortly after he was born, a young girl came to see my new baby. After looking him over, she exclaimed, "Wow! He was born that way!"

BRO. JOSE ALVES

On the east side of our house we shared a common fence with some wonderful neighbors, Jose and his wife, Aurora. He became very interested in hearing the Gospel and he received the Lord as his Savior with joy, but his wife was very much against it. Jose knew that he had the dreaded Chagas disease and wanted assurance all was well between him and his Maker. When he got that all settled in his heart, he asked to be baptized. The church marked a date for us all to go down to the Tietê River and immerse him. When he told his wife what he intended to do, she threw a fit. She threatened him in every way she knew. Finally, seeing that all she said wouldn't stop him, she delivered her ultimatum, "I will go down to the bridge then and throw myself in."

These My People

"Very well then," he calmly replied. "Let each one of us baptize himself the way he desires."

Of course she didn't follow through with her "baptism." Just to set the record straight, later on in life she too accepted the Lord and was immersed.

Slowly others were added to the church, but we felt the need to take a trip back to the States and visit our supporting churches since it had been over five years since we left. When we told the Brazilian churches our plans, Bro. Clovis said that he would be glad to work in the Pereira church so we could leave.

Returning to the States in 1963, we carried our six children who had only known life in the interior of Brazil. There were so many things of the modern world they had never seen. In Panama the coke machine fascinated them. An elderly gentleman noticed how excited they became when they saw a coke pop out of the machine if someone put in money. Then he started giving them dimes just to watch them jump up and down when a coke came tumbling out. In Houston they burned themselves on hot running water. These kids, who knew what flying was all about, didn't know much about modern conveniences. In a way they were like Brazil itself, an extreme contrast between the modern and the undeveloped. The middle ground came later with age.

CHAPTER EIGHT
Back to Jabaquara
The Revolution of 1964

THE YEAR 1964 NOT ONLY brought many changes in Brazil's history but also in the direction our lives would take thereafter. We had just returned from a trip to the States when the military took control of the country to thwart a communist takeover. In spite of some negative publicity the outside press gave Brazil at that time, it wasn't bad at all. For the next twenty years under military rule, Brazil entered into an industrial revolution which brought about modernization unequal to any other in their history. The spread of the gospel was not hindered in the least but at first we were a little anxious as to what effect it would have on our mission work.

Since our fellow workers were going back to the States for a much needed leave, we had agreed to stay in the São Paulo area while they were gone. Amazingly, they got out of the country the night before the military coup.

We had just moved into a house situated directly beneath the air lanes of the nearby International Airport of Congonhas. It was one of the most important airports in the country at that time and we could have been in the direct line of fire if hostilities broke out. Thankfully, there was no fighting, and we were relatively safe. All of the exchange banks were closed until a new government could be set up so we were caught off guard with very little money. Theoretically, we knew that God could take care of us without the American dollar, but we had to learn it experimentally.

ONE OF GOD'S SERVANTS

One day Steve went downtown to exchange our dollars for Brazilian currency but all the exchange banks were still closed. By this time we had used up nearly all of our Brazilian money. He became very hungry and decided to buy a cheap bowl of noodle soup in a little restaurant he thought was Japanese but in reality was run by Chinese. When he bowed his head to give thanks for the food, the well-dressed Oriental lady at the cash register noticed him and walked over to where he was eating.

"Do you mind if I sit down and talk to you?" she asked and then sat down when Steve said, "Please do."

"I noticed that you gave thanks for your food. Are you a Christian?"

He said, "Yes ma'am, I am. How did you know?"

She said, "Those who are not Christians do not give thanks for their food. We do. I also am a believer in Christ from China," she said and proceeded to tell how she had come to Brazil.

She and her husband, who was a brain surgeon in Communist China, fled their country when persecution against Christians broke out. They had to leave or be killed. They moved to the northern jungle of Brazil where a good number of Japanese lived on black pepper plantations and where doctors were few and far between. Since they could speak Japanese, her husband thought that he could make a living

Jeannie Montgomery

among the Japanese by practicing medicine. One evening a young man had a serious head accident, which caused a life threatening condition if he were not operated on immediately. By the light of a kerosene lamp and under the most primitive conditions, the Chinese doctor performed a successful operation on the man that night. Her husband was probably the only qualified brain surgeon in a vast area, but he had not yet been registered with the Brazilian Medical Association. After saving the man's life, his fame spread all around and this created a lot of jealousy among the doctors in the area. They had him arrested and put in jail for not having a Brazilian license to practice medicine although all of his Chinese documents were in order. Personally, it would have been better for him to let the boy die, but as a Christian he could not walk off and fail to save a life when it was in his power. That is why he operated. His family, unprepared to face the wrath of the medical profession, had to leave there to raise money for legal fees while he was in jail. They moved to São Paulo to open this little restaurant. This was the situation they were in when Steve dropped in for soup. As he finished his soup, the lady ordered the waitress to fill up his bowl again and then wouldn't let him pay for his meal. Before Steve left, she learned as much as she could about us, and promised to come visit us. The next day she showed up at our house with a big box of hot, delicious food and said that she felt led to give us some money. She didn't know we were sitting on "empty barrels." Steve had not told her that we could not get our money exchanged so were without food. We had a wonderful time with her and her son as we sang songs of praise, not in English, not in Chinese, but in Japanese. I am sorry I can not remember this person's name, but I'm sure God has it recorded with golden ink, and one day I will be able to give her a proper, "Thank you."

These My People

As things settled down on the military front, we also settled in to help the Jabaquara church while the other missionaries were away. Although a good number of new members had come into the church after we moved to the interior in 1960, many of the faces were already familiar to us. The rented building was getting pretty crowded. It had been a bar, so many of its former clients often stopped by with hopes of finding spirits of a different nature than what we had to offer. It was situated on a main thoroughfare and many people noticed our church sign as they went to and from their nearby villages. A couple of young ladies, Maria and her sister Eugenia, who were converted shortly before we came, told how they were curious about the church but were afraid to come in. Maria said they had been warned that something terrible would happen to them if they did. She feared God would send a bolt of lightening and strike her dead if she came in but she did anyway. She, with her sister and mother, became some of the most faithful members of the church and later moved to another area to help start another good church. This is how many of the new churches began. A member would move away and immediately, he or she would open up their homes for services. After a number were saved and baptized, a new church was then constituted.

JORGE AND ANESIA

During the year we were there, we became better acquainted with Anesia and her husband Jorge whom we had met on a former visit when we lived in the interior. They owned a confectionary shop and did catering for special occasions. On one of Jorge's many trips to the center of São Paulo to buy supplies, a woman of ill repute caught him by the arm and started screaming for help as if he were attacking her. A policeman, who no doubt was in cahoots with her, came running

Jeannie Montgomery

up, handcuffed Jorge, and carried him off to jail. They accused him of trying to molest her, but he stood firm and didn't let them scare him. When they saw they couldn't get any fast money out of him, the policeman threatened to call Anesia and tell her that Jorge was having an affair with another woman. Jorge calmly responded, "By all means, please do."

They surely didn't expect that answer, so they locked him up to force him to pay.

"Now, what am I going to do?" he thought. About that time he remembered the story he had learned about Paul and Silas being thrown in prison and how God sent an earthquake to free them when they sang praises to God. Jorge started singing hymns as loud as he could. The police told him to shut up, but he kept on singing. No, God didn't send an earthquake, but the police were so shaken up with his singing, they turned him loose. It certainly pays to sing when you are in trouble!

A few years ago Anesia and I were privileged to have some time together again after many years. We had a wonderful time of rejoicing and laughing about some of our past experiences. She told me about the first time she visited the church and what were her first impressions of us. On that occasion we had come from the interior to visit Jabaquara and Steve was invited to preach. Since many Brazilians had never seen a Bible, much less read one, he would explain that what he was going to say was from the Bible and that it was the only book we used in our worship. That night after he finished his introduction, he then said, "Will you now turn to the book of I Thessalonians for our text?"

Scandalized, Anesia said in her heart, "Liar! You just got through saying that the only book you used was the Bible and now you are telling us to look at a book you call I Thessalonians!"

These My People

The lack of knowledge about the Bible was tremendous at that time, partly because a good number of people could not read or write, but chiefly because those who could were forbidden by the clergy to do so! This was Anesia and Jorge's case. The State educational system was not yet well developed, so ignorance abounded. With the overthrow of the government, the military closed down many clergy run schools because they harbored communists. These schools were mostly attended by children whose parents could pay for their education, so the vast majority of common people remained illiterate. With the closure of many church run schools the burden of education fell on the State, thus great advances in the public school system were made. Even so, a great number of the adult generation missed out on a proper education; consequently, we had to deal with ignorance in every field. Fortunately, Brazil now offers many advantages in education, and the people who could not obtain a good education for themselves are able to educate their children. In our churches today there are members from all walks of life. Although there are remote areas that have been left behind in some things, Brazil is no longer what I would call a third world country. They have some of the finest experts in nearly every field of science and a good education is now more available than before.

A BROTHER FROM UP NORTH

In 1964 we still had to work with a lot of uneducated people. I never will forget how a certain brother from the North told us how he treated his parasites by taking a few drops of creosote in a glass of milk everyday. One day when he was out in the woods with his brother, he noticed an odd thing happen. He saw the mosquitoes bite him and then drop dead! It intrigued him so much, he called for his brother to come see. They noticed that the sweat on his arms stood in beads and smelled like creosote. That scared him enough to think that he might be the next to die, if he didn't stop taking it. He never told us if it cured him of his worms or not, but I bet it did.

How that brother did not manage to self-destruct, I don't know. On another occasion after he had moved to São Paulo, he got a job at the airport cleaning planes. While on the job he became ill and went to the company doctor at the airport. The doctor gave him some medicine, probably a strong sedative, in the form of a very small pill.

"Don't take more than one of these at a time every six hours," the doctor warned. He then repeated the instructions to make sure that the man understood.

As soon as this brother walked out the door, he looked at the tiny pills in his hands and thought, "These things are so small until, if one does a lot of good, two should do more so I'll just swallow all of them and get over this sickness in a hurry."

Fortunately for him, he swallowed them right there only a few feet away from the doctor's office and not at home. He walked a short distance and passed out. He was taken back to the doctor who realized what had happened and immediately had his stomach pumped out. Even so, he went into a coma and almost died.

When we were in the church at Jabaquara in 1964, the three sisters who had been Spiritualist mediums before they accepted the Lord were still faithful in church with some of their children. One of the sisters had congenital epilepsy, as did some of her children. I think at that time they were taking Phenobarbital to control their seizures, but whatever it was, they were having a hard time getting the dosage adjusted. An older daughter who was rebellious about her condition and nearly every thing else in life, left home without telling where she was going and was gone for several days. In the meantime her mother took an overdose of medicine and died. During the funeral, the wayward daughter decided to come home and was unaware that her mother had died. As she passed by our church on the way home she saw the big crowd. Her curiosity made her come in to see what was going on. While Steve was preaching, she walked up to the front to see who was in the coffin. The shock of seeing her mother there was almost too much for her. She started screaming and beating the air with her arms. Then she went over to the wall and literally tried to climb it. This disrupted the service so much that we could only get control of the crowd by singing some hymns to calm everyone down. What a pity that some families wait too long to make amends in life.

LAUREANO

On a brighter note, there was a young fellow from Paraguay who began attending church while we were in the States. We had been back to Brazil for a few months when he came to tell the church goodbye before he returned to his native land.

"I am returning home," he said, "but I am not the same as when I came to Brazil. I can never bow my knee to an image again, and I intend to follow the Lord when I get to Paraguay."

As a result of this young man's stay in São Paulo, Bro. Rogers, Bro. Ross, and Steve made a trip to Paraguay to see him about a year later. Bro. Rogers soon moved to Paraguay where a number of churches were started. It is amazing how so many of our first contacts resulted in the establishment of new churches in Brazil and Paraguay.

SISTER RITA

A missionary never knows which situation will lead to another. I can truthfully say we were never bored in Brazil; we didn't have time! The unexpected was always happening. One case in point was a church member named Rita, a sixty year old widow who was the cook and maid for my next door neighbor.

On one of her weekends off, Rita went to a town not too far from São Paulo to visit her son, who was not a believer. Before they went to bed that night, she asked him to read the Bible with her. He opened up the Bible at random to Daniel 5:25-26 and was visibly shaken when he read, "Mene, Mene, Tekel, Upharsin. God hath numbered thy kingdom and finished it." He wanted to know what that meant. In her limited way, she tried her best to explain. The very next day he was killed. Rita, who was the only believer in her family, wanted someone to read God's Word at her son's funeral. Funerals in Brazil are not like they are here. Since they rarely embalm, the body must be buried within 24 hours. She could not find a pastor anywhere and could not get word to anyone in our church. This poor distraught soul picked up her Bible, stood up, and read to the little crowd who had gathered. She didn't try to preach but was able to read and let God's Word speak for itself. It must have been an impressive scene.

DONA CAROLINA

Rita came back to São Paulo and continued her work with my neighbor, whom I shall call *Dona Carolina*. She was about thirty years old when she married a widower with two sons. Her husband and his family were some of the chief leaders in the Spiritualist cult called "Mesa Branca" or White Table. Trying to convert her to their religion, they tried every trick they knew. They took her to their séances in which her husband's dead wife, supposedly, talked to her through the medium. The dead wife sent a message to the new wife, *Dona Carolina*.

"Just wait until I get you alone, I will kill you," the medium relayed to her.

These My People

From that time on, she started having spells in which she could feel the hands of the deceased wife grip her throat, choking her. She would be unconscious for hours when this happened. Believe me, she was a pitiful, nervous woman. Spiritualists deliberately put fear into the subconscious mind of the person they wish to convert and when they "exorcise" the evil spirit, that person becomes convinced the religion is right. The Spiritualists were "slaying in the spirit" a long time before modern TV preachers learned to do it. The only difference is that one does it in the name of a dead person while the other claims to do it in the name of Jesus. Hypnotism, when not used medically, can become a tool of the Devil in any religion whether intentionally or otherwise. *Carolina* had no spiritual strength to handle her problem. On one hand she wanted to believe her husband and please him, but on the other her father did not like what they were doing to her at all. They had not managed to "cast out the spirit" so she continued to pass out.

One day when *Carolina's* husband was not at home, she had one of these spells. Rita came to the fence and called for me, "Sister Jeannie, do you want to see what Carolina looks like when she passes out?"

"Sure," I yelled back across the fence.

I dropped everything I was doing to go see what was happening. When I went in, *Carolina* was stretched out, stiff as a board, with her eyes fixed without blinking. I checked her pulse to see if it were irregular and to my surprise it was a good firm 72 beats per minute. There was absolutely nothing wrong with her. She looked like she had psychological tetanus to me. I picked up her foot and spanked it so she could feel it as I tried to reach her subconscious mind by repeating over and over again, "*Carolina*, you are not going to die."

It worked! She came to in a minute or two which was record time because she was usually out for hours. When I saw that she regained her right mind, I asked her one question, "What are you afraid of?"

Jeannie Montgomery

Her pitiful answer was, "Dona Jeannie, you don't know how afraid I am!"

She told me all about the séances her husband made her attend and how she trembled to see her brother-in-law come in the door. When she finished, I read to her how Lazarus in the Bible died and could not leave heaven where he was in peace, neither could the rich man in the torment of hell get out of there. Then I explained how that when you die, you don't go wandering around in your spirit, but stay where God puts you.

Her father, who sat there listening to all I had to say, spoke up, "*Carolina*, you listen to this woman. She is telling you the truth."

After that I gave her a Bible and told her that if at all possible not to go to those Spiritualism Centers. For some time she had no other spells. She told me that she was reading her Bible but one day her husband fooled her into going to a séance out in the country by telling her they were just going for a ride. When they came to the parking lot of the Center, she realized where he had taken her. As fear gripped her, she began to feel the cold hands closing in on her throat as before, so she prayed.

"Oh, God of Dona Jeannie and Dona Rita, please don't let me have a seizure."

As she continued to tell me what happened, she added, "Do you know what? I didn't have one, either!"

After that, her husband prohibited her from having anything to do with me or even from talking with me. Things went on in this manner for several weeks until one morning about eight o'clock we happened to meet at our adjoining gates. I noticed that a rash had broken out all over her face.

"*Carolina*, what in the world have you been eating?"

"Nothing, but I did take eight sleeping pills."

I looked again and thought, "You've got to be kidding. You wouldn't be standing here if that were so." So I dismissed it as perhaps being only a minor allergy rash.

That night I had reason to regret my swift assessment. About seven o'clock another neighbor came running to my gate and called for me to come if I wanted to see *Dona Carolina* alive.

This time I jumped into high gear and went straight to her husband. I told him what she had told me that morning and I advised him to take her to the hospital immediately since she might have taken even more pills.

Looking at me defiantly he said, " No! I have called my brother and we will handle this." (It has always puzzled me how cultists of all kinds claim to do great medical feats in Brazil, even to the point of operating, and the medical profession never attacks them as they did the Chinese man who was a genuine doctor.)

By this time the whole living room was full of women waiting to see if *Carolina* would die. Her brother-in-law, whom she feared, arrived and started the session to expel "her evil spirit." I sat there for two reasons: I knew that *Carolina* had confidence in me and that somehow she might know in her subconscious mind that I was there; the other was that I was just plain curious to see what the guy was going to do.

Taking a position at the head of her stiff body, her brother-in-law laid his hands on her head and to my surprise; started repeating the Lord's Prayer, over and over again. When he couldn't make any progress with that, he stopped and requested that we all think "protection." (Spiritualists use the power of positive thinking a lot).

That is when I spoke up. "Sir, I can not do what you are doing, but I do know how to pray."

He looked at me and said, "Sit down and shut up."

So I sat down and shut up, but I decided against leaving *Dona Carolina*.

The poor fellow had a major spiritual power failure in that session; I had broken his contact. He tried over and over again to get the Lord's Prayer to work but nothing happened. In desperation he and *Carolina's* husband picked her up and carried her upstairs to work with her alone. All the time they were carrying her up the stairs like a straight plank of wood, they were busy turning their heads from side to side to blow the evil spirits back down on us. I figured they aimed mostly at me because I was the only one who had opened her mouth; the others were either in agreement with them or were too scared to breathe a word.

At that point I realized that the devil could use God's own words as a tool if used in the wrong manner. No wonder Jesus warned us not to use vain repetition in our prayers. This principle no doubt works in singing as well.

About mid-night the brothers came downstairs. By this time I figured some of the drugs had worn off. When *Carolina* started moving, they said that we could now go up to see her.

When I walked over to her bed, she looked up and in a strange deep voice started talking as she turned her head back and forth, "You think this is me talking but it is not."

I claim no special powers for then or now. In fact, I had not even prayed, when she looked at me again, and blew out a big puff of air after which she became extremely weak but completely normal.

I learned from this episode in Spiritualism that if a true believer in Jesus comes in among them, they cannot function. There is no reason to be afraid of them.

These My People

OUR BELOVED BROTHER, DR. RACY

Toward the end of our stay in São Paulo, we met Dr. Felix Racy, who became a lifetime friend and co-worker. Shortly after his birth his family brought him to Brazil. They were given 24 hours to evacuate their enormous estate in Lebanon when the State of Israel was being formed. Having accumulated a sizable fortune in Lebanon, his grandfather became one the founders of the American University in Beirut. In Brazil his family established the Racy Industries of Brazil. Dr. Racy was being educated and groomed to take over his family's business when he became a believer. Refusing to take over the leadership of the company because he wanted to dedicate his life to serve God, he entered medical school and became a medical doctor. After finishing his studies in Brazil, he worked at Baylor Hospital in Dallas for three years before returning to Brazil to pursue his desire to be a medical missionary. Unfortunately, after he and his wife returned to Brazil, serious marital problems separated them. To his eternal honor, he chose not to remarry for the "kingdom of heaven's sake." I have never seen anywhere a more sincere and honest man in all of my life. He chose to give up all the family riches and dedicate himself to live with the poor and treat them. This man, who was literally raised with a silver spoon in his mouth, now lives like a pauper in his old age because he chose to work among the poor.

A BROTHER FROM JAPAN

About six months before we moved back to the interior, a young Japanese man we had never met left the church in Tokyo to come help us in the mission work in Brazil. We thought he intended to preach to the Japanese in Brazil, but that wasn't his idea at all. He stayed with us for several months until he moved in with a Japanese family in another area where Bro. Ross was working.

While he was at our house, I felt sorry for him since he had never left his homeland before and I would cook a Japanese dish several times a week so the food change wouldn't be too hard for him. Anytime a person abruptly changes his eating habits, he is subject to getting sick. The few oriental dishes I knew how to cook were those I had learned from Japanese women in Japan, so I knew what I cooked was the real thing. That is why it always puzzled me why he never once said "Thank you," or "That's delicious," or "I'm surprised you know how to cook Japanese food." Apparently he just didn't believe in praising the cook for trying to please him. I only found out what he really thought about my cooking one day after he had left us to live with a Brazilian-Japanese family. The wife told me he reprimanded her because she was Japanese but "could not cook good Japanese food like Sis. Jeannie, and she is not even Japanese." By this time I could not appreciate his roundabout compliments. My sympathy was totally for her.

While living with them he decided to move to the southern part of Brazil and work with only Brazilians. Not too long after he moved there, he became interested in a Brazilian school teacher who was trying to teach him Portuguese. It was always a puzzle to us how he managed to propose to her, since he could not speak the language. But marry they did! Love knows no barriers; even though his mission work never got off the ground, his marriage had a flying start. I pray that God may yet use him.

Toward the end of our year in São Paulo, Dr. Racy moved to a little interior town called Santa Cruz do Rio Pardo. After Bro. Rogers and Bro. Ross returned to Brazil, we were free to move on to other fields. Our hearts once again sought God's will as to where we should work. Steve made several trips to the interior looking at different places. Dr.

Racy invited us to come work where he had located. Finally, we settled on moving to Santa Cruz do Rio Pardo. This town would become what my children think of as "home."

CHAPTER NINE
Santa Cruz Do Rio Pardo
A New Door Opens
1965-1977

Santo Cruz do Rio Pardo is a town where, as the locals put it, "If you sneeze on one side of the town, the other side knows you have the flu." In other words, there are no secrets here and when you hear the news, it may be exaggerated. The strong Italian influence is tangible everywhere. Fair blue-eyed children, whose grandparents came from Northern Italy, played in the streets. With the abolishment of slavery in Brazil the need for farm hands was great so a lot of Italians colonized this area when Brazil opened her doors to more immigrants at the beginning of the twentieth century.

As we drew near the town on Good Friday of 1965, Steve pondered out loud, "How can we really know if God wants us to move to Santa Cruz do Rio Pardo or not? He doesn't send a telegram from heaven."

Both Steve and I laughed at the thought of God sending us a telegram from heaven, telling us to go here or there. Our conversation was very much on what decision to make as we approached Dr. Felix Racy's house. He had invited us to come look over the possibilities of starting a church in this area and we had attempted to do so several

These My People

times but could not find a place to live. We came to the conclusion that if God wanted us there He would give us a positive answer to our prayers about it on this trip. Because communication was difficult at that time, Bro. Felix did not know when, or even if, we would be there. Before we left São Paulo, our prayer had been for God to show us definitely His will by arranging not only a house to live in but also a meeting place for us to hold services. If those two things were arranged on this trip, then we would feel that it was His will for us to move there.

Driving up to Dr. Felix's front porch, we could see the surprise on his face as he jumped up from his chair to meet us. "I tried to send you a telegram but couldn't because the office is closed on Good Friday. I found you a house with a separate room over the garage where you can start services," were the first things he said.

Steve and I looked at each other. God CAN send a telegram from heaven by way of Santa Cruz do Rio Pardo if He so desires!

The house was everything that we wanted. The only drawback was it was located right on the backside of the Sao Benedito Square where one of the town's two major Churches was situated. Nevertheless, we reasoned that if this is what God had arranged for us, then this is where we wanted to be. We believe very much in the providential leadership of God, so we made final arrangements to move. Shortly afterward we arrived there with our belongings. By this time, Dr. Felix also had moved to another village called Ubirajara, where he desired to open up his practice and start a church.

May 5, 1965 was a lovely day for settling in our new house. The truck with our things was already there when we arrived at dawn. Having a lot of work to do made no difference to my small children. When they got hungry, they wanted to eat. Around seven o'clock with the children clamoring for breakfast, I had to take out time to go look for a bakery.

As I started around the block, I encountered an old woman with one shoe on and with the other in her hand. (I didn't know it at the time but soon found out she had dementia and lived in the corner house near us with her husband Antonio.) She tugged at my arm and said, "Where's Antonio?" She didn't want to let me go but I escaped as I managed to loose myself from her grip and say, "He's probably over there."

A little while after breakfast, someone clapped her hands at the gate. (This is a Brazilian custom which takes the place of a knock or doorbell.) An elderly couple on the corner sent their maid with a pot of beans because they noticed that we had several children and thought they might be hungry. Later in the day when I returned the empty pan, the maid ushered me in to meet the lady of the house. Immediately, the lady informed me that I shouldn't pay too much attention to what the maid said because she was feebleminded. When the old lady stepped into another room, her husband came in and his first words were to warn me that his wife's mind was not quite right. Before I left, all three had advised me about the precarious mental state of one another. Returning home I saw a young man picking grass from around a concrete post in front of our house. While I was wondering why he was doing that, he spoke up and said, "I have to get all of the grass cleaned from around this post so it won't catch the plaza on fire." In the house I said to Steve, "Honey, let's get out of here while the getting is good. I'm beginning to wonder if everybody in town is a bit loony and somehow it may be catching." Of course this was not the case. Santa Cruz was an educational center for a large area and some very brilliant minds lived there. We just happened to move near some deficient people.

These My People

A week after we moved into our new home, Steve had to take a week's trip to Rio de Janeiro. Alone with the six children and in a strange town, I became apprehensive. What would happen to the kids if I got sick? Or if one of them got sick? I didn't know anyone in the whole town. If something happened to Steve, what would I do because I didn't know my way around? In all my years on the mission field I never let my children know when I was afraid so I had not opened my mouth once. Inside me my fears built up until the Lord sent me a little messenger to sit on my lap. Cuddled in my arms my two year old baby who didn't know what he was saying, looked up at me and said, "Mommy, God hold you like you hold me." My mouth dropped. I cried because I was so weak and faithless that God had to use the mouth of a baby to correct me. I knew that my salvation was an eternal gift, once and for all time, but my daily walk by faith should be my way of life. There are days it's almost gone and others when it's big enough to move mountains, but this was one of my weaker days. After I received my rebuke, I straightened up and told God, "Thank you, I'll behave now." (By the way, my baby was no spiritual prodigy; neither was Balaam's donkey. God uses many different ways to get to us). After Steve returned, we began our regular church services. The town did not welcome us with open arms; no one came. People went out of their way *not* to meet us and turned their heads when we were near. This place promised to be one hard place to work. After ten months of door to door evangelism and no outward results, we began to wonder if we had erred in understanding God's will for us to be here. We knew that sometimes God lets you go to one place in order to get you to another. Our prayers were always for God to lead us to the place we should be. Finally, one of our neighbors that we didn't know very well came to church.

SEBASTIANA

Sebastiana was a middle-aged lady who taught catechism classes in the local church. She was very curious to know what Steve was preaching. For months she took her crochet and sat on a stump in the churchyard directly in front of our window where we were having services. If anyone wondered what she was doing, outwardly she was only crocheting in a cool place, but inwardly she was listening to the gospel. Without our knowing what was going on, the Lord was working mightily in her heart. When she was saved, she came up the stairs to tell us all about it.

We were so happy. Surely the Lord was now going to start working in earnest. Evidently, this was where we should be, but another eleven months passed with no visible results from our constant evangelism. Steve then began a daily radio program and decided we should open up another meeting place in a different part of town.

The new meeting place was located in what was known as "Little Mexico." Why it was called that I do not know, but I do know it was one of the roughest areas in town. The only place we could find to rent was an old bar. It was large enough to hold a good number of chairs so we cleaned it up and were in business.

This time the crowds came. The radio program was beginning to have an effect and people were curious to hear more of what that "Gringo" had to say. We held a week of nightly meetings with Bro. Ross preaching.

One night a big strong man came in and sat down. As Bro. Ross began to preach, the man shook his hand in the air and shouted, "That's a lie!" After several of these interruptions, Steve, who did not even come to the height of his shoulders, walked over to him, took him by the arm, and asked him to come outside with him. Immediately, several men jumped up and went out to see if the fellow was going to beat Steve up or not. The guy was a known assassin who worked at the local slaughter house, handling heavy carcasses. The men knew Steve didn't stand a chance of walking off on his own two feet.

"Sir," Steve said to him, "you are in no condition to attend our church services now, but we would love to have you come back tomorrow night when you are not drinking. Be sure to bring your family, too." Steve's request completely took him off guard leaving him docile. To everyone's surprise, he turned and walked off. What surprised us most was that he actually came back the next night with his family. After church he told the men that he had been sent the night before to cut the tires on our cars and cause havoc. "But," he said, "something just didn't let me do that."

FRANCISCO AND FAMILY

Francisco, an elderly gentleman who listened to Steve's program every day, had a large family who dabbled in spiritualism. He liked what Steve had to say about the Bible and told his family, "If you want to hear God's Word, go to that American's meeting." He was ill and could not attend at first, but his son Morel and family did. The Lord did a work, not only in Morel's heart; but also in his wife's and they were saved. After the meeting his dad was able to come to church. He and his wife, Teresa, were also added to our number of believers. Soon there were several candidates for baptism. This was the boost we so desperately needed. Our place to baptize was at the entrance of the town. A bridge spanned the Pardo River at a point which had an easy access to the water. When our group gathered and began to sing, the bridge above us loaded up with a large number of curious people. Most of them had never seen a baptism like that of Jesus and John the Baptist in the Jordan River. When Steve started to baptize Bro. Francisco, the heckling began. "You're going to kill the old man. You're going to kill the old man!" they chanted in unison from the bridge.

Bro. Francisco heard what they were saying, and calmly told Steve, "I can't talk very loud so will you tell them this old man is already dead! This is just the burial!" The nucleus of a new church was rapidly coming together and we were able to organize the first Baptist Church of Santa Cruz do Rio Pardo. Members were added regularly. We started services on the other side of town also. Our months of waiting were vindicated. It pays to wait on the Lord.

Most of Bro. Francisco's family later trusted the Lord. His family has become our family. Morel's daughter, Isabel, is now my own daughter-in-law. From his family we now have pastors, deacons, and faithful followers of the Lord in the work in Brazil. Morel's father-in-law, Joaõ, was a big, tall, rawboned Italian whose parents immigrated from northern Italy. Joaõ was a very religious person who led in the home prayers (chanting) of his church somewhere nearly every week. When he heard that Morel and his daughter Lourdes had become a part of us, he vowed that he would never put his foot inside our church. But one night we had preaching services at Morel's house and Lourdes asked her dad to come. He rebelled at first but later decided he needed to see what we were doing. Noticing that Steve had brought the kids and me with him, he decided that it could not be too bad if a man could bring his family to such a gathering. That made him listen. Before he left the services that night, the Lord had done a great work in his heart. Without Steve preaching against drinking and other sins common to Brazilian men, Bro. Joaõ quit his habits and came to church faithfully until the day he died.

The Lord began to add to our number almost daily. About that time a young man, Antonio, who from then until this day we consider

These My People

to be one of our family, came into our church. He has been faithful in all his ways and helped tremendously in the work in Santa Cruz, Pereira Barreto and for the last seven years, has been the pastor of a church in Bauru.

After a couple of years in the house we rented, our landlord wanted his house for his wife's parents to live in. We were able to buy a place on the opposite side of town. This proved to be a blessing since the house had a huge double garage ideal for converting into a meeting place. The local junior and senior high schools were almost in front of our house and the grammar school was only a couple of blocks farther away, so we were very well located for our needs. Since I was not one of those super moms who seem to have time to do all the right things, I knew that if my children got an education, I had to send them to public school. My new house was conveniently located for me to put them in school which I learned was a very good one. People began to learn who we were and didn't seem so afraid of us, although until this day there are some people in town who declare that we were CIA agents. Even our neighbor next door to us told one of our church members just before we moved away that it was a shame that we were CIA agents because we were such good neighbors.

With the children in school, things started to happen. I was soon known as David and Tim's mother or Steve's wife. I often wondered if people knew I had a name. Not long after we had moved to our new house, a large circus set up its tents directly across the street from us. Knowing my four boys as I did, I tried to lay down a few rules with number one being: don't get close to the lion's cage. Before long the kids came home singing the news, "Michael pulled the lion's tail! Michael pulled the lion's tail!" God has always taken care of us, not because of us but in spite of us. At an off hour for the circus workers, Steve made

Jeannie Montgomery

them a visit to pass out gospel tracts. One lady was deeply touched. She said, "No one has ever taken interest in our spiritual welfare before."

Having six children at home, I had my own three-ring circus to contend with everyday. All were in public school with normal growing problems. On one or two occasions a little persecution occurred because we were Americans. The day Robert Kennedy was killed, David was beaten up on the school grounds in front of the teacher, who did nothing to stop it. The Kennedys were idolized in Brazil at that time, and all non-Catholic Americans were blamed for their deaths. As they beat David, the kids chanted, "You Americans killed Kennedy." The beating didn't do any great harm to David and by the next day he was ready to go back to school. On another occasion Timothy had some strong caustic solution squirted into his eye at Carnival time. We had to rush him to a doctor in another town over fifty miles away for specialized treatment. Mercifully, God spared his eye from going blind. This time Steve looked up the father of the young boy who had hurt Tim. The fellow wanted to pass it off as nothing and thought Steve had come to get money out of him. Steve let him know that he didn't want his money at all, but he did want him to keep his son from doing the same thing to another child. At that time there was unrest in the town and the military got wind of what happened. They asked Steve to open up a law suit so they could go into the school and check them out. Steve refused to do so, so the case was closed.

On a whole our children adapted to Brazilian schools without a problem. We laugh at our own government here in the States for thinking you can not have an official language in the schools. Children can learn any number of languages at the same time and know to whom they should speak which. Because there is an innate desire to be like those around them, children will pick up the local language quickly. At home we made our kids speak English to help them not forget English.

These My People

We also had them take turns at reading the English Bible in our daily devotions. I guess you could say that the Bible was their English reader. In school and in the street they learned Portuguese like a native. So much so until if they wanted to say something mean to one another, they did it in Portuguese because they had not been taught how to use bad language in English at home.

Shortly after moving to our new location, Morel's brother, Waldemar, came into our work. Waldemar had one big problem; he was afraid to let his wife know that he had been converted. Whatever he did at church, he had to slip around and do it. His dad, Bro. Francisco, became very ill again and Waldemar carried him to his house to take care of him. That gave Steve and me a chance to make a visit in their home. When we went in, Waldemar's wife was no-where to be seen. Steve went into the bedroom to read and pray with Bro. Francisco and I went to the kitchen to talk with his wife, Sis. Teresa. She told me how Francisco wanted to die and be with the Lord. I commented on how the apostle Paul said in the Word of God that it was far better to depart and be with the Lord than to remain in this life. About that time from out on the back porch, a high pitched voice screeched out, "The Word of the Lord! The Word of the Lord! That's all I can hear around here." Although I didn't see her face, I knew it was Waldemar's wife. We left without seeing her, but after her in-laws returned to their own house, she went to their first house service. She went to the bedroom which opened into the living room and stayed there with her baby. When the preaching service was over, Steve gave an invitation and out she came! She has been in the church ever since. At that time she didn't know that she was to become the future pastor's wife!

UBIRAJARA

In addition to our church work in Santa Cruz we were going to Ubirajara twice every week. In fact, we were able to organize a church there before we could in Santa Cruz. Ubirajara, a little village tucked away among coffee farms, was so far off the beaten path until if you didn't know how to get there, you would never find it by reading a map. Dr. Felix chose this village because no doctor bothered to live there.

We had some very interesting times in the work in this place.

TERTULINO

One of the first converts was a village drunk, Tertulino. He was taken to Dr. Felix's office when he had a mild stroke. Steve had gone there for mid-week services so Dr. Felix asked Steve to take him back to Santa Cruz with him and intern him in the hospital. A few days passed and Steve went by to check on the old man. To his surprise he had simply disappeared. Alarmed, Steve went by the police station to report the missing man since the hospital personnel had not done so and did not want to be bothered. Steve initiated a search of his own without any luck. A couple of days passed when he had to walk about five or six blocks to get a hoe sharpened. There sitting on the sidewalk was an old gray-headed man with his head bent down in his hands. Steve spoke to him and soon saw that it was Tertulino but he was totally out of his head. Tertulino invited him to "come in and have a cup of coffee." He didn't know anything that was going on. Steve came home, got our car, and took him to the police station to let them know Tertulino had been found. That's when the fun began. The very incompetent sheriff tried to put Steve in jail for kidnapping him. It took a lot of persuading for him to decide that Steve was trying to help the old man. Then the sheriff took them all back to the hospital and demanded that the personnel tell him why they had let him get out in the first place. This particular sheriff was famous for being hot-headed. The town gave him the nickname of *"Bronquinho,"* which means "The Little Tirade," because he was always bawling out someone.

Tertulino regained his mind and went home, never more to drink. He was saved, cleaned himself up, and God changed his life totally until the day he died. He now has four generations of his descendants in the church serving God. One of his sons is a pretty good poet and has written lyrics for hymns.

The one thing I most remember about Tertulino is how he was baptized. We all went down to the creek at the edge of town where Steve led him into the water. Steve kept trying to lay him backwards in the way we usually baptize and he wouldn't go. Realizing that the man thought he had to go forward, Steve changed his direction of baptism and buried him face first. What difference does it make as long as you get him under? The word then got out that the difference between us and another church in town was that we baptized forward and they, backwards.

A TINY WOMAN

On another occasion when Steve went to Ubirajara, he found Dr. Felix very perplexed about a patient to whom he had given a "horse" dose of sedative. A tiny little woman, who did not respond to the medicine, was very wild. She saw Steve, whom had never seen her before, and tried to get up off the table and get him. It took four big men to hold her down on the examining table. Dr. Felix told Steve in English, "This woman has nothing wrong with her. Evidently her problem is a spiritual one. Would you please pray for God to handle this?"

Without ceremony Steve simply asked God to remove the problem and as soon as he finished she gave a deep sigh and went to sleep. After she had slept two days, she told how she had gotten angry with God when she went to the Mass to pray that morning. Then in a fit of rage she gave herself to the devil, and "this thing" came over her.

OTHERS WHO CAME

On another occasion a couple of young sisters started coming to church without their Daddy knowing it. When he learned about it, he was so angry, he went to confront Dr. Felix and warn him about what he planned to do. "I don't want to ever see you again, but if I do, I'll beat you up."

The very next day his bull gored him so badly, the family had to bring him to Dr. Felix. He saw Dr. Felix a lot sooner than he planned. It was he who got the beating from a bull! He learned not to get in the ring with a heavy weight.

Amid all these unusual happenings, the Lord added to the number of believers so that we could organize the Ubirajara Baptist Church. The night we chose to officially declare ourselves a church, about twenty-five of us went to the organization in three vehicles, two VW vans and a VW bug. Going over there on the forty mile stretch of dirt road we had good weather, but while we were in church, a storm came up. The roads turned into a traveler's nightmare. On the way back all three vehicles got stuck three times each. That was nine times the men dug out the cars so we could go a few miles farther. Finally, we came to a mud hole and the front car got stuck. It was impossible to move or for the others to go around it. We all resigned ourselves to sleeping piled up against each other in the cars while we waited for dawn to arrive. When we could see a little, the men noticed a tractor parked at the top of the hill. Hurray! Help was in sight. Santa Cruz was just over the hill! We all got to our house in time for me to fix a big breakfast before we crashed.

Adorcina, the wife of the first Japanese we baptized in Brazil, had come for the occasion. She confined to me that before she came from Sao Paulo, she had prayed that God would let her see what it was like to be a missionary's wife. I looked at her and laughed, "You are the culprit for us having to spend the night on the road. Now you know what it's like."

God always has a plan for things which happen in a Christian's life. *Sebastiana's* husband, *José Lino*, who was not a believer when he went with us on that trip, came back a truly converted one. What impressed and made him examine what we taught was to see all the grown men get out in the mud, get their nice clothes muddy, and laugh and sing as they worked with each car. When he got home he told his wife, he had never seen men who would not have cursed and gotten angry at what we all went through that night. He wanted to know more about what made them different.

Another door was opened not long after we organized the Ubirajara Church.

RIBEIRÃO DOS CUBAS

Because of the radio program many of the farm people heard about our church services and a large group from about fifteen miles away started attending. They also asked us to start services out in the farm area where they lived. Many of them owned their own farms and had peons who worked for them. From the start we had large crowds and

Jeannie Montgomery

the Word was well received. Some still thought that the earth was flat and that men going to the moon was Hollywood fiction.

The group prospered and built a meeting place. but since nearly all of them were related, family problems soon came in and destroyed the harmony that had been so sweet. One brother's cows got into another brother's corn. Instead of solving the problem at home, they waited to get in front of the church and have it out with each other. The church demanded that both parties repent, but neither gave in an inch and were excluded. One brother moved his church membership to another town but the other one became ill with cancer and died shortly afterwards. Before he died, he called for the Elders and got his life straightened out with God. He had a remarkable death. Because he was in such pain, the family requested that Steve ask God to give him peace and take him on home to Himself. That was the first time Steve had ever prayed a prayer like that, but he did. As soon as he finished, the brother gave a sigh of relief, smiled, and then slowly stopped breathing. The pain and sorrow were over; he was in the presence of the Lord.

Most of the members in Ribeirão dos Cubas came back to the church in Santa Cruz when all of this happened and gave up trying to be a church of their own out in the country. We did have some good times out there while it lasted. One brother and his wife were always such a sweet blessing to us.

BRO. EDSON

When we first met Edson, he and his family lived in a little unpainted wood house that looked like the wind could blow it away any minute. He did very well on his farm and decided to build a big brick house. The very day that he moved in the new house and got all of his things out of his old house, it collapsed.

Someone said to him, "It's a good thing you got out of that house when you did or it would have fallen on you." His reply was, "No, it could only fall when we moved out." Just a matter of how you look at life!

Bro. Edson and his wife were faithful until the day they died.

A YOUNG GIRL FROM RIBEIRÃO

Once a young girl came to visit us from Ribeirão dos Cubas and decided to spend the night with my girls. During her stay we had to do some extensive house cleaning so she jumped right in to help. She was poor and I wanted to give her something for her work but she refused. Then I went to the store and bought a big sack of candy for her to take home to her siblings. To my surprise she refused that too. Her reasoning was odd. "If I take this candy home, then my brothers and sisters will like it and will get used to it. We are too poor to buy candy for them, and if they want it real bad and we can't get any, they will get the *"febre de vontade"* (fever of desire). I was to learn that nearly all Brazilians believed that if you want something really bad, you will get sick if you do not get it and could even die from wanting it. This was a dreaded disease which children could always use to their great advantage. I explained to my children that it would not do them any good if they came down with this "plague" because I would not change my mind and I would probably let them die. (Although they were always wanting something, none of them ever had fever from it).

If all sicknesses were as easy to treat as this so-called fever of desire, we never would have to worry; however, illness did come without advance warning.

Jeannie Montgomery

TIMOTHY'S SICKNESS

Timmy came in one day with a stomach ache and fever. Checking him out, I saw right away he needed a doctor. Steve carried him across the block to a small hospital served by two or three doctors. Dr. Kalil thought Tim had appendicitis and immediately made arrangements for the operation. In the middle of the operation he called Steve to come to the operating room. We knew something was terribly wrong. When they opened Tim up, they found that his lymph nodes were swollen. Things didn't look good for our twelve year old son who had not yet trusted the Lord to save him. Dr. Kalil took out a couple of nodes and sent them to a big hospital in Sao Paulo for testing. In the meantime, Tim had his appendix out and was hooked up with a constant penicillin drip. That first night, his fever rose extremely high. Because the hospital was so small, the night nurse decided to take a nap and did not respond to my constant buzzing. I began to panic. By that time I was ready to break into the nurse's station and get some medicine myself. Since I couldn't get in the station, I thought about going home to get some, but I knew that if I left the hospital, the door would lock after me, and Timmy would be left alone. Earlier, Steve had gone home to the other small children. I couldn't call him because we didn't have a telephone. I gave up trying to rouse the nurse; in fact, I didn't even know where she was. I went back to Tim's room. I did the only two things I knew to do, pray and bathe him with cold towels all night long. At dawn, a sleepy eyed nurse came in to check on him. Somehow I managed to keep my cool but when the doctor made his round, he got a full report of the night's happenings. I think maybe the poor nurse did not get to sleep on the job from then on.

The report from Sao Paulo showed that Timmy had generalized lymphadenitis. He was not responding to treatment like he should.

For days Steve and I were concerned about his spiritual condition if he were to die. Weary and heartsick I went home for rest. Steve took my place and talked to him about his soul. He acted like he had not heard and dropped off to sleep. When he woke up, he raised his arm that wasn't tied down with tubes and quietly said, "Daddy, I'm trusting Jesus now." Until then I think even he felt that he was going to die, but at that point his health began to improve. Still the source of his infection was not known. His fever left and the doctor let us take him home. He was so emaciated, his dad picked him up like a small child. A few days later I examined his teeth and found what looked to be a pinpoint cavity. At the dentist's office the doctor started to drill and found the whole tooth was only a shell. The source of his infection was located!

Life returned to normal or rather to our normal way of doing things. I'm of the firm conviction that if God calls a person for a job, He equips him to do just that. It is when someone says God told them to do something which He never commanded, that trouble comes.

A YOUNG MAN BRINGS TROUBLE

Trouble moved in one day with most of his things in the form of a young man who said he had come to help us in the mission work. We did not know him very well but since he came from one of the churches we began, we welcomed him and did everything possible to settle him into the work. As time progressed I began to have a gnawing thought that I would not let myself admit. Most of his clothing told me that he probably had an alternate lifestyle. Some others had said so but in my mind I tried to ignore it, thinking that he just wanted to look modern and different. He knew the Bible very well, but I could never really be edified by what he said. After a year or so with us, he became interested in a young school teacher in our church and decided to marry her. As soon as their second child was born, his wife became sick with venereal disease. Confusion broke loose in the church. With his marriage in ruins, he confessed to being a homosexual and unfaithful to his wife. No one wanted to believe it, but the facts were there. From a very reliable source we learned that when he was young, he and several other young boys frequented the home of a priest noted for this kind of lifestyle. While we believe very much that if a person who commits any type of fornication can be forgiven, we also believe that if they repent they can and will change their lifestyle. Repentance is the key. May I add that in our dealings with these people, nearly all were introduced to that lifestyle by someone they admired and who was a lot older than themselves.

Missionaries will sooner or later have to deal with all kinds of situations that aren't pleasant and can almost tear up a young fragile church. If he will just hold steady and trust in God, things have a way of calming down. Thank the Good Lord, these crises are the exception, not the general rule. In the end our church lost the whole family but the church itself began to grow again. Fortunately, difficult times are not for ever and wonderful things were always just around the corner.

I always thought that deaf people were a quiet bunch of people until I saw several young women going down the street using the sign language but making all kinds of odd noises as they gesticulated to each other. The thought that I would soon be racking my brain over how to communicate with them never crossed my mind.

MARIA LUIZA

Maria Luiza came to us one day to get us to translate a letter she had written to a friend in Canada. The contents of the letter went

These My People

against our beliefs and I didn't feel comfortable writing it for her. There was one big problem; Maria was deaf. How do you explain everything to a deaf person when you don't know the sign language? When Steve was young, he preached to deaf people in Arkansas, but each country has its own system of communicating and Arkansas sign language didn't quite fill the bill in Brazil. Besides that, he had forgotten many of the signs he knew. Maria had studied four years in a deaf school which was more than most deaf people in Brazil have a chance to do. With Steve's help, a pencil, and paper we managed to understand a few things. It didn't take long to perceive that her ignorance in general was appalling. At that time the common person in Brazil equated being deaf to being mentally deficient, therefore families did not even bother to educate them. When she asked me to teach her the Bible, I had a formidable job, which without God's help I could do nothing. I was totally ignorant of the sign language, but I did have one advantage; I could read and understand Portuguese. Portuguese was still a foreign language to her. Since she could not hear anything I might say, my American accent didn't hinder our study. Besides my learning how to communicate with her, I also had to teach her Portuguese as I taught the meaning of every other word in the Bible.

The very next day she was at my door as soon as lunch was over and we worked together from three to four hours everyday from then on. If she knew a sign, she taught me, and then in turn, I took the sign and used it to explain another word. Both of our vocabularies grew. Our lessons went something like this: Gen.1:1 "In the beginning" (she stopped me and signed a question to know what the word "beginning" meant. To explain that, I lined up a bunch of matches and picked up the first one. This went on with other visible objects until she got the meaning). Her next word was "created." At that point we went out in the yard and I poured water on a pile of dirt and made a mud man.

Jeannie Montgomery

Until we both could learn better, the sign for "to make" became our sign for created. By the time she left me in the evening, my imagination was totally exhausted. At the same time we were in Genesis, I decided if she ever learned enough to be saved, I would have to start in Matthew as well. During all of this, she came to church without missing a service. Although I could not translate to her, I would point in the Bible for her to follow along in the Scripture Reading.

Apparently, God was making her understand more and more everyday. Repetition was an absolute necessity. After about four months, she came to our study smiling with the incredible news that at church the night before she had asked God to forgive her of all of her sins. She made the sign for peace in her heart!

By the time Easter came around that year, we had just finished the story of the resurrection. Good Friday is always a day of mourning in Brazil because they believe that God is dead that day. A person should not do anything like work, sing, or make noise, and especially be happy. (The chicken thieves took advantage of this day; since God is dead, He would not see them stealing.) Bubbling over with her new found faith that Jesus was not dead, Maria Luiza tried to sing. Believe me, when a deaf person tries to sing, the sounds that come out are sometimes unrecognizable. Her mother heard her singing and reprimanded her severely because, she said, "God is dead." Maria looked at her mother and shook her head and said, "No, Mother. God is not dead, He is alive, and he rose again. That's why I am happy!"

When we began to understand and communicate better with each other, I began to perceive the deep feelings deaf people have. She told me once what all deaf people wanted most in life was to be accepted by others as normal human beings.

Years later when I saw Maria, she thanked me for everything and then commented as tears ran down her face, "I don't know why God

These My People

choose to let me be the only one in my family who has accepted the Lord. They all can hear and read but do not want to hear God's Word. I am deaf, but He let me hear His Gospel!"

My daughter, Deborah, and Bro. Waldemar's daughter, Marie, learned the sign language so they could talk with Maria Luiza. She became so efficient she could translate the church services for Maria. Several months later Maria Luiza moved to Sao Paulo and attended classes in the sign language Bro. Gardner gave to preachers and workers. He told Steve that Maria knew more Bible than any deaf person he knew. God certainly did a wonderful work in Maria's life. Now she can even say several things audibly to people who do not understand the sign language.

MADRE MATILDA

God doesn't just work on one front. New people came into our lives constantly. I like to remember the nun, Madre Matilda. (Her other name given when she took her vows I'll not reveal). She came to me one day to ask me to teach her English. At first I didn't really care about doing that but I reconsidered and arranged classes three times a week for her. We got along fabulously. Sooner or later our discussions would turn to the Bible. She told me that only three years prior to her coming to me that the Vatican allowed them to begin reading the Bible. Before that, it was prohibited. Our lessons progressed for some time, and then one day she didn't show up. After about two week's absence, she returned.

"You'll never know what happened to me," she explained. "I was in a wreck. Our chauffeur hit a mud hole too hard and it turned the jeep over, throwing me out. There's one thing I want you to know, while I was rolling over and over in that mud, I was praying to Jesus and not to my saints. When I got home, I told my sisters that it wasn't any saint that saved my life. It was Jesus!"

"You're on the right path, Matilda. Keep it up," I replied.

I'm sorry to say that immediately after that visit, Madre Matilda was transferred and I never saw her again, but I often wonder if she really knows that Jesus saves from more than physical harm. I hope she remembers to read I Timothy 2:5 "For there is one God, and one mediator between God and men, the man Christ Jesus," and believes it.

STEVE GETS HIS WINGS

Steve, the father of six children, decided he wanted to get his pilot's license. It seemed that he was spending too much time on long trips to areas where a plane would facilitate his work without wasting time. He enrolled in an air club in Ourinhos, a town about 22 miles from Santa Cruz, where they gave flying lessons. It required permission from the Aeronautical department of the federal government for him to even enroll. After all the red-tape was taken care of plus many trips to the club for lessons, Steve finally soloed. When a person solos for the first time in Brazil, he gets an oil bath. The other pilots pour buckets of burnt oil over him as he kneels in the vat where they store the used motor oil. The candidate usually provides liquor for all who partake in this oil bath, but we carried them cake and cokes instead.

After all of this and passing the written test, the club's president then had to personally present him to the federal agent who gave the flight test. The club's president was none other than a federal congressman in the Brazilian government.

OUR CONGRESSMAN

On one of his many trips back home to our area, our district's congressman was to drive Steve to Presidente Prudente to take his flight test which had to be given by a federal examiner from Rio de Janeiro. Getting up early Steve noticed that the day promised to be very rainy which would cancel the flight, but he insisted on going anyway since the federal government had told him to appear. The congressman let Steve know in no uncertain terms that he felt it would all be in vain for them to go because of rain all over the State. Steve felt that if the Lord were in it, the weather would clear up enough to fly so he wouldn't give up on going. Arriving at the airport at the correct time, they noticed that the only place where the weather was open was near the airport! Even the examiner was not able to fly in but had to come by bus. With seventeen students from several air clubs waiting their turn to earn their wings, each one wondered who would go first because it was evident that the airport would soon close down. The instructor had never seen Steve before but looked square at him and said, "You go first." After Steve proved his ability to maneuver the plane, the rain closed in on the airport. After a hurried landing and before they could get the plane tied down, the rain began to pour down. He was the only one that day to take his test. On the way home, our congressman marveled, "Mr. Steve, your saint is a lot stronger than my saint."

Steve responded, "That is because my saint is the only true God." He had a wonderful opportunity to talk to him about Jesus.

Through him, Steve met other high officials in the government.

When the time came for Steve to officially receive his license, this congressman sent his Mercedes over to our town to pick Steve up for the occasion. Steve had the distinct privilege of being the first U.S. citizen to earn his license in Brazil, or at least that was the announcement on the Voice of America. Other Americans had their Brazilian licenses, but they had learned to fly elsewhere, not in Brazil.

Steve was able to secure an old Cessna at a good price in California. With the help of a retired pilot of United Airlines he flew it down to Brazil.

God has all types of servants who have their own special places in God's scheme of things. Bro. Savage, an elderly gentleman, was one of those unique ones.

BRO. SAVAGE

Retired from United Airlines he certainly had some interesting stories to tell. When World War II ended, the highlight of his career was to fly home many of the survivors of the famous Bataan Death March. His own brother, Colonel Columbus Savage, was among those he brought home. With pride he told how his brother worked on the chicken farm in the prison camp and was able to help save many of his men from starvation. He would make a small hole in both ends of the eggs he gathered, blow them into his empty canteen and later give them to fellow inmates. To dispose of the shells he merely ate them. (I bet his teeth never rotted!)

Bro. Clarence, as we called him, stayed with us about three months which was long enough for me to get an idea of what he thought. Apparently, he believed that the women in the Bible always symbolized evil. (With him in my house I honestly tried to put on my best behavior so as not to give him more reason to confirm that, but I doubt it changed a thing.) He had his own health code which didn't include going to the dentist. We became very concerned about his health when he woke up with fever one morning. Upon questioning him, we found that he had a serious tooth cyst that needed attention. He informed us that he had not been to a dentist in twenty-five years and had no intentions of going to one. I remembered our son's near death and prayed that nothing would happen while he was in our care. Thankfully, the fever left him.

Our children watched with interest when they saw him eat bananas. When he had finished, he would take his knife and scrape the inside of the peeling. He said he was getting a rare vitamin that way. He must have done something right because he lived a long life and died years later, not of sickness but from an airplane crash. He faithfully served God in his own way.

With so many new things coming into our circle, life promised to be full. There are dates in a family's history which divide time as "before and after." The year 1973 was that for us.

1973 A CLIMACTIC YEAR

The year started off calm enough without a hint as to how it would end. David entered his second year of college in Brazil and the other five children returned to school. The Potters, who had come to Brazil to help in the mission work, settled in next door with their two young children. It seemed we were in for a stretch of peaceful living with everything going "story book" fine, but it was only the calm before the storm.

Our church planned a week's revival in May with Bro. Pires, an ex-priest, doing the preaching. The week before he came, for reasons known only to God, our American money did not come in and we were flat broke without food. At church on Wednesday night Steve preached on 1 Kings 17: 9-16 about how during a drought a widow was about to use the last bit of meal she had to bake a cake for her and her son, when Elijah came and asked her to make it for him. Knowing that the meal was the only thing between her and starvation, she did not question the prophet's request but did as he commanded. God took care of her and her son by multiplying her supply until the drought was over.

A BOX OF CORNSTARCH

As he preached I sat on the bench laughing to myself: What in the world did I have in my pantry that God was going to multiply so we could eat? I thought I didn't have a thing. When church was over, I went straight to the cabinets and of all things to find was a big box of cornstarch, roughly four and an half pounds, and about a pound of sugar. From there I looked in the refrigerator and found three eggs and a small amount of butter. Immediately, a simple Brazilian recipe for one of their favorite muffins came to mind.

You guessed it! The next day my kitchen became a muffin factory with my kids working as topnotch salesmen. We were extremely blessed by God. Not one muffin broke even though these muffins break easily. They all sold as fast as I could make them. When I got enough money, we stocked up on material to make more muffins and there was also enough to buy some food for the day. This went on for about a week making us wonder what was going on between us and God. I thought that surely I could close down my factory any day, but it was not to be that easy. Bro. Pires came and to be sure he would be well fed, I went to each lady in the church and asked if she would like to have him over for a meal. We were too embarrassed to admit to the people that we didn't have any money. Our fare was soup. When the weekend came, the Lord sent us a car load of young people from Sao Paulo to help us eat our "bounty." With one chicken to stretch between twenty-five of us, I prayed for the Lord to multiply my food. Making as much stock as I could and then taking the chicken off the bones, I made corn bread dressing for an army. That plus a salad and spaghetti with a Jell-O dessert was our meal. When everyone finished, I could hardly believe the amount of food we had left over for supper. God CAN furnish a table in the wilderness!

David came to me on the next Saturday saying, "Mama, I feel so bad. I should be making money to help us." To this I replied, "Son, go clean up your room, then kneel down and ask God to give you something to do." He closed his door and after a little while came out when he heard someone clap his hands at our gate. A group of five students had come to get David to tutor them in English for an upcoming test. That produced the grand sum of five dollars for the weekend, but more importantly, it produced more faith in our son who was about to go out into the world on his own. His comments to me after our trial was over were, "Mama, all this happened for my sake".

After another week went by, Timmy said, "Mama, you want to know something? The day God sends us money, you won't be able to sell another muffin." A few days later I made muffins as usual, but the kids could not sell one of them. That was the day money came! And WE ate muffins!

I look back on that month as God's school to teach us and our children that He can supply all of our needs even if He has to multiply a box of cornstarch. "Great Is Thy Faithfulness" became our theme song as we gathered around the piano to sing each night. "Give us this day our daily bread," had new meaning to us. It wasn't just a prayer to be repeated, but an assurance that God does control our needs, and supplies them.

After that trial of faith it seemed that God opened up the gates of heaven to bless us. We settled back into a normal life. In the meantime David received a scholarship from Letourneau College beginning in September of that year. Our attention went to getting our firstborn off to school. Until that time, I never felt it a sacrifice to be on the mission field, but when my own child is a continent away, the heartache is so tremendous.

Life continued, but 1973 was not going away without trying every fiber of our being again.

VISITORS FROM THE U.S.

December rolled around. Unexpectedly, a family from the States showed up on our steps needing a friendly hand. Thinking that land in Brazil was cheap, they had come to buy a farm to get their children away from the evil influence back home. My house was like our VW van, it had the heart of a mother with room for one more person, so they moved in, all five of them. They were a joy to have, but it didn't take very long for them to find out that farm land was extremely high and out of reach. After looking around for land for three weeks they decided to give up living in Brazil and to return home.

TWO FUNERALS

Before Steve carried them to Sao Paulo to catch the plane the day after Christmas, we had a busy week. Old Bro. Francisco died. During the funeral Francisco's little five year old grand daughter was playing near a fire in the yard and squirted a bottle of alcohol into the fire. She was seriously burned when the bottle exploded. She lingered for a few days then died. Two weeks before she died her other grandparents had taken her to church where she heard for the first time the old hymn, "When The Roll Is Called Up Yonder". She liked it so much, she sang it constantly until the day she died. Her parents, who were not believers, asked us to conduct the services and sing that song. When we arrived at their home we learned that a group of objectors who were relatives planned to throw us out. We did not want to cause any trouble for the grieving parents so we conducted the services at the grave site where no one could object. Until this day when I hear or sing that song, I remember the little girl who has already heard the roll call. A blessing came of this tragedy: her mother became a faithful believer.

Sometimes things happens so fast, there is hardly any time to rest. Steve carried our new friends back to Sao Paulo to catch their flight, and as for me, I picked up a book, went out in the back yard, and propped my feet up with full intentions of doing nothing but reading a whole book. Since the trip to Sao Paulo took seven hours, one way, I looked forward to pampering number one.

THE ACCIDENT

Sitting on the lawn chair without a care in this life I could hear the traffic going by on the street in front of our house when all of a sudden I realized someone was clapping. Going around the house I could see two strange men standing at my gate. It was six o'clock in the evening and I wondered what they wanted.

"Lady, are you Steve Montgomery's wife?"

"Yes."

"Well, we came to tell you that your husband had a wreck and is in the hospital at *Tatum*. He just had a few scratches, but is alright. Perhaps you ought to go see about him."

I had been in Brazil long enough to know that when a person is either dead or in a serious state, the relatives are told that they should go see about their kin in the hospital instead of just saying outright what the problem is. At that point I didn't know if Steve were dead or alive. They assured me that he was alive but to find out how bad the wreck really was I asked, "Can I go drive the car back?"

"No, Senhora, the car is totally demolished."

I thanked them and they left. Now the problem was to find a way for me to go to Steve. Without resources of my own, no car or money since Steve had carried our American money to exchange it, I contacted Bro. Waldemar. He, his son, and his daughter came and as soon as we could get our things together, we left. One look at Waldemar's pale face made me wonder if he were going to be able to drive all the way. Since he was my way to Steve, I tried to not show any emotion but to encourage him. "Waldemar, Steve is in God's hands and we can't do anything about it, so let's just leave him there." When he saw he didn't have to handle a hysterical woman, he was alright.

We walked into Steve's room at midnight, twelve hours after the accident, and could see that something was seriously wrong. His neck was swollen straight down from his chin, and he was talking nonstop as if his life depended upon it. Shattered glass had perforated his whole neck area and barely missed his main arteries. At that hour of the night I couldn't see the doctor so we left to find a place to sleep. But first we had to go to the police station. Looking at the wrecked car parked in their yard made me nauseated. The hood had come all the way in and cut the seat on the passenger's side. If I had been with him, I would have been decapitated. On the driver's side it had wrapped around the steering wheel, which saved Steve's life. Steve told me that the money he had exchanged in Sao Paulo was in his brief case in the trunk of the car. The trunk had not been damaged so everything there should have been intact. I knew better than to expect to find the money. Also, so as not to accuse the police of taking anything and to keep me from getting into trouble, I looked the police in the eye and ticked off what I should find before he took the key and opened it. That way I let him know he wasn't fooling me. Just as I expected, the money was gone.

These My People

One more time I was without money and had no where to lay my head. The hospital manager looked up a Baptist church and asked them to let me sleep with them that night. May God bless the couple who opened their doors to this stranger! Next day the hospital put Steve in a private room with a guest bed for me. We stayed there in that hospital a week. By the end of the week the churches in Sao Paulo had heard about what happened and they all gathered up offerings to help us. When the time came to pay our bill, they had given enough to handle all of the expenses. Yes, I love these people and am eternally grateful for them loving us as their very own!

Just before we left, the nun came into the room to give us her last instructions. She said that we should massage his neck and have him to turn his neck as much and as often as possible!

Fortunately, the pain would not let him turn his neck at all. Stupid me, I had not asked to see the x-rays in the hospital but had taken their word for everything. I did remember to ask for the x-rays to take home with me. After we got home, I called Dr. *Moco*, a friend of ours, and showed him the x-rays. We were amazed to see that Steve had four cervical vertebrae broken. Why he was still alive and not paralyzed was beyond all belief. If he had followed the instructions given him in the hospital, he would have died instantly. Sometimes pain can be a blessing.

Dr. Moco arranged for me to take Steve to a hospital in Ourinhos where Dr. Flavio was an orthopedic surgeon. He immediately wanted to admit Steve for surgery to attach a halo for putting him in traction. The stay would be for an indefinite length of time. While the offerings from Sao Paulo took care of the first hospital bill, I was once more without money. By that time being without money was getting to be a chronic situation with us. What we were about to face would require a lot more money than the first hospital had asked. The head of the hospital came around to inform me that they would not accept Steve without a two thousand dollar deposit. When the personnel left, in despair I walked out in the hall, slid down the wall to the floor, and for the first time since the wreck, lost my composure. That was the way Bro. Waldemar found me. When all help seems gone, God is not without resources. Good ole' Waldemar came to my rescue again!

THE BEST BROTHER A PERSON COULD HAVE

Surprised to see me slumped down on the floor, he asked "Sister, what's the matter?" When I had told him our situation, he asked me not to worry because he would arrange the money. With his help we managed to get things in order and get Steve admitted. Again I am humbled by the generosity of this great brother. (The reader might like to know that Waldemar later became the first Brazilian pastor of the Santa Cruz Baptist Church and served faithfully as such until the day the Lord called him home.) He has a special place in our hearts.

FAMILY IN A CRISIS

As soon as the doctor could rig up a halo, which he himself had to make, Steve was carried into surgery. When they had finished and had brought him back to the room, the doctor looked at me and said, "You lift his head while we put him on the bed." I didn't hesitate because we had come this far without me even knowing his neck was broken. What was wrong with me handling Steve one more time, if God still had everything in control?

There was no modern equipment in the hospital, not even a suction machine in the room. His bed was a plain flat cotton mattress with only an extremely thin pillow under his head. To the halo they attached little sacks of sand to hang down at the head to stretch his neck. That was it for twenty-one days.

As he began to regain his consciousness, the excruciating pain was not relieved even with medicine. We had a long, long night. All night Steve prayed for God to let him die. I was almost to the breaking point when I decided to argue with him, "Don't you dare die."

"You can get along fine without me. You're still young and can get married again."

At that I retorted with a laugh, "What man in his right mind would want to marry a forty year old woman with five kids at home? No, Sir, don't you dare die."

Daylight couldn't come soon enough for me. Without a suction tube, I had to take a towel every time he gagged, and clean out his mouth. He could not turn his head or body a fraction of an inch to one side or the other so he could vomit. I feared that he would strangle to death.

The doctor came around the next morning and adjusted Steve's sand bags. This gave him some relief. When Bro. Potter came in, Tim and I left to get some rest. There comes a time that the primary caretaker has to get away and recoup before she or he can be useful again.

At home I found another problem. Michael Ray had fallen on a stob and had injured his ankle. It seemed that trouble would never stop coming. The doctor said that there was no major damage done and bound it up. Later I thought that perhaps God had done a favor by "hobbling" my mischievous son so as not to give too much trouble to the Ross family who had come to take the kids home with them. If I had known that the doctor was wrong and that a big piece of the stob was still in his ankle, I would have worried. But what you don't know doesn't hurt you, so for the time being I was at ease about going back to the hospital.

Settling in for an undetermined length of time I tried to make the best of the situation. People were always sticking their heads in the door to get a glaze of "that American" with a broken neck. Their gasps and exclamations about how horrible Steve's problem was didn't bother me after awhile. On a few occasions people actually came by for us to pray for them. About the only time I nearly jumped out of my skin was when a fellow stuck his head through our window and yelled, "Isabel." I assumed he was calling his girl friend who worked there.

Steve remained three weeks in the exact position we had put him the first night after the operation. Finally the day came when the doctor decided to put a collar on him and let him up. When the attendants wheeled him back to the room after putting on the collar, Steve was so anxious to sit up, he wanted to go straight to the chair. Against my advice to take it easy, the nurses sat him up and walked out of the room. They no more than got out of the room when Steve began to faint. I called the nurse back and she asked me to help her put him back into the bed. I said, "No, ma'am. You go get help". I knew she and I couldn't move dead weight, and if he were not dead already, we might just finish killing him. She hurried out and got an orderly but by the time she got to the door she could see that Steve's eyes had rolled to the side in a fixed deadly manner. Death was written all over his face. That is when she screamed for Dr. Flavio. He came running and put me out of the room to work on Steve. When they got Steve in the bed, and had revived him, I was allowed back into the room. Alone with the doctor near Steve's bed my nerves felt like over-tightened guitar strings ready to pop. The doctor asked me what I thought had happened. I told him that I thought Steve had had a blood clot. In true spiritualistic fashion, he said, "You can't think that way."

Before I knew what I was doing, I gave him a punch on his upper arm and replied, "I can if I want to. Now you listen to me, don't ever

These My People

let a patient like Steve get up without gradually raising and lowering his position until he adjusts. I knew he would pass out."

Surprised that I had done such a thing, I regained my composure and behaved from then on. Honestly, Dr. Flavio is a wonderful doctor, and I behaved shamefully under the stress.

A week later the good doctor put a Minerva jacket on Steve. It is a body cast. So with Steve looking like an astronaut we were able to bring him back to the States by the end of January. On the trip back on one of Braniff Airlines' last flights, we made two stops and at each stop all seven of us were shuffled around all over the plane. The company's seating "system" was totally messed up all around. In Panama Steve was asked to sit in the back of the plane near some Brazilian pilots who were going to the U.S. to ferry planes back to Brazil.

A big cowboy type American got on the plane demanding his rights. Walking back to the Brazilian pilots he informed them that they had his family's seats and that they must get up and let them have their rightful places.

The men didn't budge. "No, Sir, we have been sitting here since Sao Paulo and we are not going to move." Things heated up so the stewardess came and asked the "Ugly American" to be seated in another place. At that point Steve managed to stand up and ask the American to take his seat because it had three in a row and would accommodate the family. Grumbling they settled down after the pilot almost threw them off the plane. Under his breath the trouble maker could be heard to say, "That guy got his fool neck broken and just wants our sympathy."

Steve waited a little until we were in flight, then with difficulty got up again, went back to the cowboy, and calmly told him that he knew how he felt because he had six of his own family scattered all over the plane. He then quoted James 1:20, "For the wrath of man worketh not the righteousness of God," and turned and went back to his seat. Under his breath the cowboy was heard to ask, "Who is that man?"

Amazingly, Steve came out of the cast after about two months and then was put into a more comfortable neck brace. After four more months he was free of every support without being crippled. Only God's grace can do a thing like that!

After about a year of recuperating we were able to return to Brazil and continue our work. This time we left Timothy in Louisiana. (Missionary wives have asked me about when to leave children in the States. I honestly don't know. Each child is different and the need to be with parents may vary).

Back in Brazil we settled into the work once more. Bro. Potter decided he should work in the Madeira Islands and had already left. With two of my own gone and the Potters also gone my American family dwindled, but my Brazilian family grew larger.

While we were in the U.S., an American missionary who was not of our fellowship, bamboozled the Santa Cruz Church into letting him use the airplane in "his work." Soon after we returned, a Brazilian Air Force official, who knew Steve well, met him and told him that the so-called missionary had used our airplane to smuggle precious stones to other countries, hiding them in the plane's spare tire. The military did not take action and seize the plane only because they respected Steve and our church. The plane had been registered in the church's name. Evidently the missionary thought that Steve would never be able to return to Brazil so he took full advantage of the plane. We got the plane back just before the man skipped the country. The plane was almost stripped of everything inside and was in a sad state. Considering everything that had happened, we decided to sell the plane and use the money to help build the Pereira Barreto Church.

AN AIRPLANE MECHANIC

An English friend owned an aircraft maintenance shop in Botucatu where Steve took our plane for servicing. One day this man flew a customer's plane to a town in Paraná, just south of us and was to be back before dark. (It is not legal to land a plane without instruments at night in an uncontrolled airport). His only option to land was the airport in Ourinhos for it was the only one in the area with lights. He left for home later than planned so he decided to land and overnight there, but suddenly realized he did not have the documents for the borrowed plane and it was fast growing dark. He couldn't go back or all the way home without being illegal but he couldn't land in Ourinhos either without paying a fine. So he decided to land on the airstrip in Santa Cruz and overnight with us. He followed a small river which turned out to be the wrong one. When he arrived at another small town, not Santa Cruz, he saw what he thought was the dirt strip but was really a plowed field. Right after touchdown he flipped over, but was not hurt. He then hitched a ride to our town and spent the rest of the night with us. He called home and his wife brought his workers with her, arriving at our house about five o'clock that morning. I put her to bed while the others went to dismantle the plane and load it on a truck. When he and Steve returned the next day to get the plane, rumors were already flying. They stopped for gas and the station owner, not knowing he was talking to the pilot himself said that the pilot was trying to pick up a rancher's daughter to elope with her. He reported that others thought the pilot just needed to go to the bathroom! He said he wasn't sure which was correct. Steve and our pilot friend didn't bother to enlighten him. Later another story got started that it was Steve who wrecked the plane. Finally the rumors stopped and life again returned to normal. Sometime later, when Bro. Waldemar was ordained to be the pastor,

Jeannie Montgomery

our work was finished in Santa Cruz do Rio Pardo. Pereira Barreto needed our help and we felt we should move back there.

CHAPTER TEN
Pereira Barreto
1977-1990

Both of the churches in Pereira Barreto and Sud Menucci (the new name for Pioneiros) were without pastors, and the people were clamoring for us to come back. We felt the need was great enough to return; our time was divided between the two places. There are only about twenty-five miles between the two towns so we moved back to Pereira in our former house. It was like coming home with one exception; four of our children were in the States. The comfortable old house was half empty now. I knew that the remaining time with my children was precious and there was yet much work the Lord had for us to do here.

We had been away from this region for a long time and there were several new faces in the churches. At Sud, the short name for Sud Menucci, we met Bro. Pedro and Sis. Maria before they moved farther west to the nearby town of Ilha Solteira. They became frequent names is our household.

Jeannie Montgomery

MARIA AND PEDRO

Maria was always laughing. I could see that she had something terrible happen to her leg in the past, but even when she told me about that, she had me laughing before she finished. They had not been married but a few years when Pedro brought home a gun. He didn't have the least idea how to handle the thing so he began checking it out. Somehow or other he pointed the gun down at her leg and it went off by mistake. In the confusion a neighbor called the police who hauled Pedro off to jail. Maria, with her leg needing attention, had to beg the police to let him go so he could take care of their babies. She had to assure them over and again that he did not shoot her intentionally before they would release him and she could go to the hospital. I have known her about forty years and she still carries fragments of lead in her shin bone but I promise you that even though he shot his wife, they were a happily married couple until the day he died.

They gave Rebekah and Steven a very special little puppy who soon won our hearts and ran our household. As soon as daylight came she would run into our bedroom, tug on Steve's hand, and drag out his running shoes. That would always get him up for their morning run. It was because of these daily exercises, Steve found the local Japanese ball park where several elderly people came to walk early each morning. He began to make laps with a gentleman who was a Buddhist.

A LOCAL BUSINESS MAN

Akisui San was an esteemed member of the Japanese society and owned a big farm equipment store. After they became friends, Steve told him that we had just lost a grandchild and how that we would yet see this child when the resurrection came. He was so impressed he

These My People

said, "I admire you Christians. My religion is good to live by but not to die by."

A few years later when we returned from a trip to the States, we heard that while we were gone, he suffered a stroke and could not talk. Steve went to visit him and as soon as he went in, Akisui San saw who it was and lifted his good hand to point to heaven, and said only one word, "Jesus." He then pointed to his heart and smiled. That was a precious moment. A mutual friend told us later that Akisui San had become a Christian before he had his stroke. He did not live long after Steve's visit. At his funeral our friend, who was very important in the Japanese community, told the hundreds of Japanese who were there the unknown story of how Akisui San had found peace and eternal life in Christ Jesus the Lord.

I'm glad we went to Brazil!

The majority of Japanese did not seem interested in hearing about Jesus. There is a popular sect among them called, "*Seicho No Ie*" or House of Wisdom. It was started in Japan in 1930 and we heard of it while in Japan. When the Japanese immigrants came to Brazil, they brought this religion with them as well as Buddhism and Shintoism. This new religion teaches that all religions have some good and bad in them and that their religion held the knowledge of what part of each was right. To them Jesus was only one of the many ways to God. We always contended that if what Jesus said is not totally true, then He is not worthy to be believed in any point. He said, "I am THE way, THE truth, and THE life: no man cometh to the Father, but by me." If Jesus spoke the truth, then there are no other ways to God. We stand on the veracity of His declaration without any apology. Of necessity that makes any other way wrong. We met many Japanese who adhered to their way of thinking and tried to just take what is "good" from each religion and adapt it for themselves.

Jeannie Montgomery

Along with these new acquaintances we renewed our friendship with local friends we knew from the first time we lived there.

DR. ALVARO

The same day we moved back to Pereira, a young doctor also returned to his home town to set up his practice. When we lived here before, Alvaro was in his last year of high school and preparing to take his college entrance exam. English was a required subject so he came to us to help him learn it. Now, fourteen years later, we find ourselves moving back into the same city. Providentially, our paths had crossed again. Although he never came into our church, he became a wonderful friend who never tired of talking about the Bible. Many times he would pass by our house on his way home from work just to discuss with us some of the things that bothered him or some issue of the day. That was good because we were kept informed about what was going on around us.

When the second largest hydroelectric dam in South American was to be built near Pereira Barreto, Dr. Alvaro told us about the town meeting in which the first plans for this huge endeavor were made. Among the councilmen present was one illiterate soul who really excelled in ignorance. The engineers were discussing the problem of how the law of gravity would cause a problem with the flow of water.

The councilman then stood up and said, "Gentlemen, if the law of gravity is a problem, I propose that we make an amendment to change that law" How simple that would be!

During our absence from Pereira, fourteen years had made many differences. Although there were still many undereducated people, the tendency was to get a good education and this helped to balance out the population. This area was gradually catching up with the rest of the country.

While we were living in Santa Cruz, a new bus station was built only a half a block from our house in Pereira. Our block was sandwiched in between the police station and the bus station. This caused a constant stream of people passing by our house, and beggars were everyday visitors. By this time, twenty years after we first arrived in Brazil, we knew how to sort out who were the professional beggars and those who honestly needed help. Some were interesting people.

MY FAVORITE DRUNKARD, DITO

Not very long after we moved back, I noticed a guy walking down the middle of the street. If a car or an animal drawn cart came by, he immediately assumed the role of traffic cop, either signaling for them to go around him or to come to a stop. At least he managed to keep them from hitting him. It didn't take very long for him to discover our house because it was right in the middle of his "patrolled area." He came by almost daily.

When I learned his story from some church members, I didn't mind giving him a plate of food any time he came by. At one time he was considered the best brick layer around and though he was not converted, he donated his skill to help build the church house in Pioneiros. When his wife died, it threw him into deep depression making him seek solace in the bottle. Benedito, or Dito as we knew him, had never trusted the God of all comfort to fill his void. Years passed, and the liquor took its toll. I saw how debilitated he had become once when he asked for uncooked food and a pan to cook it in so he wouldn't be a bother to me. Of course, I saw right through him; the food and the pan would be sold for liquor and never reach his stomach. I gave him a little sermon and told him to come back the next morning without drinking and I would see what could be done for him. I really didn't expect him to come, but he did; bright and early. His body was in such a state of tremors, I knew he could not live long. I not only gave him breakfast, I let him have some raw rice.

The next time I saw him he had a different request, "Oh, Dona Maria (it's common for all women to be called Miss Mary), would you please give me a Bible?" I had already been warned that if a drunkard asks for a Bible, not to give it to him because he would sell it for liquor. This time I felt compelled to tell him that the Bible said that no drunkard will inherit the kingdom of heaven but that Jesus could change his destination if he would only trust Him. One of the most vivid mental images I have of Brazil is what happened next. He bowed his head and said, "Pray for me, Miss Mary," turned around, and walked off. That was the last time I ever saw him. He was found dead in the bus station within a few days. My heart mourned for him. Had I done all I could have for this poor unfortunate being?

PAULA

Shortly after we moved back to Pereira, I was taught a very humiliating lesson by one of God's precious, ignorant people. When Paula paid me a visit, I made an attempt to "get down" on her level. I asked how she made couscous from *manioc* meal. She started telling me how to make it, and then all of sudden, she stopped and looked at me, and said, "My! There are a lot of things you don't know yet, Sister!"

She was so right! From her I learned a few lessons she didn't even know she was teaching me. First, I don't "get down" to another's level; I'm probably already there or below them. Next, no matter how well educated a person may be, he or she can still be ignorant of many things. Also, we should be ready to learn from anyone. (My reader probably doesn't know how to make couscous of *manioc*, either. See there, there is still a lot you don't know yet!)

She still had one more lesson to teach me. When I served her something sweet on a paper napkin, she carefully opened up the napkin and tore off one-fourth of it for herself then handed me back the other part. "Here, Sister, you can save this; I don't need it." How wasteful I felt all of a sudden!

Before she left and without her knowing what was happening in my heart, I felt guilty of a lot of sins I didn't even know I had. Thanks, Sis. Paula, for a wonderful enlightening visit!

A NEIGHBOR

On the opposite corner from the police station I had a neighbor whose way of living left much to be desired. The need to tell her about how Jesus forgives and cleans up a person's life helped me decide to pay her a visit. Trying to be as tactful as I could without saying, "Lady, get your life cleaned up or you're not going to make it to the pearly gates," I said, "As for myself I need a Savior." Then I proceeded to tell her about how Jesus forgave my sins. My confession shocked her so much, I could almost read her mind! "What had this American preacher's wife done?" Quickly raising herself above my low state of degradation she told me that she had never sinned. OK! That put me in my place and nothing I said impressed her. I went home looking and feeling like a terrible sinner.

SEBASTIAO'S PARROT

One night Steve went to visit the home of a church member named Sebastião, and as was his custom when he got ready to leave, he had prayer with the family. As he was finishing his prayer and was saying "in the name of Jesus," he heard someone say a loud, "Amen." It came from under the table! The family's parrot had given his benediction. It made us wonder how many Americans had parrots who knew to say amen at just the right time when someone prayed.

SO WHITE IT'S SCARY

Most of the people who were not Japanese in Pereira had come from the northeastern part of Brazil to work on the dam construction. They were the descendants of African slaves who were in the Northeast in great numbers when slavery ended. Many had not been around white people very much. At first, they didn't know how to take me, but gradually I was accepted as one of them. I didn't really realize just how much until one day a sister commented to me about a white man, "He is so white, so white, it scares you!" She did not even realize that I was white. That's when I knew I was no longer a complete outsider.

ARLINDO AND EMANUELA

When we moved back to Pereira, *Arlindo* and *Emanuela* were already in the church. We didn't know anything about them. After Steve preached on marriage and how Christians should be legally married instead of just living together or practicing common law marriage, (there were many common law marriages at the time), Arlindo immediately decided to marry the woman he had lived with for thirty years and get things right with God and the country. Within two weeks they gathered all their kids and grandkids for a party to celebrate their wedding. They were so overjoyed, we wondered why in the world they had waited so long.

These My People

Neither of them was in good health. Arlindo had one of the biggest varicose ulcers I had ever seen in my life. It went nearly all around his leg in a three inch band. He was in pain night and day. Out of pity I asked him if he would let me come everyday to dress his sore because evidently he didn't know how. The doctor had given him a prescription which he could not buy. Since he had a prescription, I wasn't afraid of getting into trouble if I treated him. For forty-five days I went regularly and had the joy of seeing that monstrous hole gradually close in with skin. It was hard to believe that it healed without a skin graft. When he went back to the doctor, the doctor was surprised. For the first and only time in my life, I got a letter of thanks from a doctor for accomplishing an almost hopeless job. (Don't ever rule out the real factor: God.)

While I was making these daily visits, Emanuela opened up and told me her life's story. She started off by saying, "Sister, my life has been a *novela* (Soap Opera)." When she finished, I would have called it more of a nightmare than anything exciting like a novel. She told how she had lived with this man and that man, but finally ended up the last thirty years with Arlindo. But what stuck with me was when she finished, she sighed and said, "You want to know something? I thought I would never find peace but I have at last found it." It is at moments like this I'm thankful we went to Brazil.

There were other cases very much like Arlindo's and Emanuela's. We have married couples and at the same time registered their kids for birth certificates.

APARECIDA

Aparecida, a grandmother with a large number of children and grandchildren, was another case that came into the church without anyone knowing her legal status. At the end of a lady's Bible class in which we studied how all couples should be legally married and should not live in a common law state, she came to me and said, "I need to talk to you." She came to my house the next day and instead of being contrite over her situation, she was overjoyed at the thought that she might have a good reason for not staying with her old man! She asked me if I had an extra bed so she wouldn't have to sleep with him. "Hold it, Sister," I said. "That is not the way you handle this situation. You already have a big family; just stay put. Get your marriage legalized." It wasn't long until there was another big family celebration which took care of the marital problem.

CARMEN

As Steve was preaching one night, we noticed that a very troubled young lady had slipped into one of the church pews. His subject about hell shook her. Sooner or later everyone who dabbles in Spiritualism is tormented, sometimes to the point of despair. Before she came in, she was on her way to commit suicide, when she heard us singing hymns. She was a medium who had become so disturbed by the spirits she was working with, that she began to think that the only way out would be to kill herself. Upon hearing the sermon she decided that death would be like jumping out of the frying pan into the fire. She listened very intently to the Gospel. Embracing salvation, she was freed from her awful sins and their torment, and went home a happy person.

GRANDMA BARBARA

If you have ever seen Grandma on "The Beverley Hillbillies," you have seen what Grandma Barbara looked like, clothes and all. Her granddaughter told me it took six yards of material to make one dress for her and then nearly the same amount for each layer of underclothes she wore. This tiny little toothpick of a woman was the essence of modesty. At ninety years old she still maintained her house and could shame a lot of us younger women when it comes to housekeeping.

She was extremely religious with images in every corner until one day she began to observe the lives of all of her children and grandchildren. There was such a difference between her grandson and his family, who were members of our church, and her other children, until she decided she wanted what they had before she died. She turned to the living God and threw out all of her idols. After that she came to visit us.

Sitting demurely on the couch beside her grandson she felt compelled to advise us of her chronic condition of "dried up intestines" before she could get down to the real reason for her visit. I honestly thought she had come to get us to pray for her constipation problem, when in reality all she wanted was to tell us she had been converted and wanted to be baptized. After she went before the church and professed her new found faith, we took her down to the Tietê River, which was on the edge of town, and baptized her. As was our custom, we ladies rigged up a shelter for changing clothes by forming a circle with each lady holding up a part of the blankets to provide privacy. When Grandma Barbara started taking off her clothes, she threw each piece over the top of the blankets. The pile grew and grew until we all wondered if it were possible for her to throw any more. Grandma was modest indeed!

DR. ANTONIO PIRES

Dr. Antonio Pires is without a doubt one of the most distinguished and learned persons we have ever had the privilege of having in our home. He had been with us once before in Santa Cruz do Rio Pardo, but at that time I never had the time to just sit down and learn at his feet. I didn't want to miss out on anything this time. Once he started talking, I pushed everything aside and listened until he stopped. This great man had a wonderful story to tell of God's grace.

He left home in Portugal to become a priest while yet young. One of his colleagues and good friends at the seminary where he interned was none other than the nephew of the Bishop of one of the poorest parishes in Portugal. Distressed at his uncle's plight, his nephew, according to what Dr. Pires told us, concocted a plan to make his uncle rich. He begged his uncle to give him leave from school long enough to implement a plan to bring in a steady flow of funds. The famous story of "Our Lady of Fatima" was now about to unfold, not by divine origin, but by a very earthly fabrication made by a fun-loving youthful priest. Here is the account not told in religious circles.

Knowing that some poor ignorant little shepherd girls would pass by on their way to and from the pastures around noon, the young priest had his sister, *Rosa*, to dress up as the Virgin Mary. He helped her up to the top of a certain tree beside their path and then positioned himself where he could not be seen but where he could reflect the sun with a mirror on Rosa as they approached. The children were very frightened when they saw the light flashing, but Rosa calmed them down by saying that she was "Our Lady" with a message for them. They were to return at a certain time when she would reappear and give them some important messages for the future. They immediately spread the news in the village and at the appointed time of "Our Lady's" return appearance, all of the people came out to see the spectacle. By that time, the Bishop, who was privy to the scheme, had to restrain the people so they wouldn't get too close. At this time "Our Lady" gave the children some supposedly important words of prophecy that were to be revealed in the future. Bro. Pires said that these children were not allowed to stay in the village any longer after this and were cloistered

These My People

away until their deaths. Notice that these children really did see what they believed to be the Virgin Mary. They really did hear what she said.

Just like his fellow seminarian had planned, the area became famous and money flowed in as it became a worldwide tourist attraction. The myth of "Our Lady of Fatima" known around the world was born, but Bro. Pires insisted that she should be known as Rosa and not Fatima. By the way, he said that Rosa was a wonderful cook.

Bro. Pires earned several doctorates with his specialty being Canon Law. During World War II he was the Vatican's radio spokesman in the Portuguese language. He was closely connected to Pope Pius XII and was the personal secretary of the Archbishop of Braga of Portugal (who had the same status as cardinal.) It was because of the death of this bishop that Bro. Pires left the Catholic Church.

The Bishop of Braga was a great man. He gave to the poor and really tried to save himself by his good works. Bro. Pires said that unlike himself and others in the priesthood, this man was very good. The bishop got sick and the doctor told him he had only a few hours to live. Upon hearing this, he started begging for someone to tell him how to save his soul. No one could give him any assurance. He died crying, "I'm going to hell. I'm going to hell."

This shook Bro. Pires to the core. If this good and honest man was going to hell, where would he end up? He knew he wasn't good. After the death of his beloved friend, he was given the task of interviewing over a thousand nuns and priests for the purpose of placing them in schools across Italy. He decided that after he had finished the interviews with each, he would privately ask them the simple question, "If you were to die tonight, do you have assurance that you will go to heaven?"

The results shocked him. Not one of them gave him an affirmative answer. No one knew. He decided that there was something basically wrong with a religion in which none of its leaders had any assurance as to where they were going after death. He asked leave from the Vatican to go back to Portugal to rest.

Back home in Portugal, he dedicated himself to reading the forgotten book, The Bible. There he found the answers to eternal life that he longed for and gave himself to the Lord. When the local priest got wind that Bro. Pires had changed, he asked him to come say the Mass the next Sunday. When he did not go, the police were notified and an ultimatum was issued for him to say mass the following week. Upon his refusal, he was carried to jail and tortured. This was during the reign of the dictator, Salazar. When they turned him loose, they again gave him a date to come say the mass. Bro. Pires knew he had to get out of Portugal, so he went to his house and packed his bag, and in the dark of the night walked as far as he could. He then got a bus to cross the border into Spain. He remembered that his Vatican passport was still valid so he immediately booked a flight to Brazil where at least there was religious tolerance and all Portuguese citizens could get in freely without a problem.

Once in Brazil, he started studying all the religions that his church had classified as heretics to see what they believed. He found that of all of those listed, the Baptists believed more like he understood the Bible to teach so he began looking for a Baptist church. Our contact with him came about when both he and Steve met at an ordination service a few years later. It was at that meeting Bro. Pires learned that his prayers for a church to be started in Santa Cruz do Rio Pardo were answered. His wife, an ex-nun, was from there.

DARCY

A few months before Bro. Pires visited us in Pereira Barreto, the local college asked me to teach a course in English to an advanced class in the American Cultural Union. The Brazilians have a saying that "in the land of the blind a one-eyed man is king." That adage surely fit me because I was not an English teacher. I did have an advantage over them, though; I knew the English language fairly well as my very own. After praying about it, I accepted the challenge.

As I stood at the entrance of the classroom the first day to welcome each student as they arrived, I saw a short, roly-poly, loud, middle-aged woman come bouncing in. She told me her name was Darcy and said enough words in English for me to sum her up to be a nervous, chain-smoking Portuguese. Something in me was drawn to this insecure woman although she tried very hard to give the impression of being a very self-disciplined person. I could tell that she came from an educated background but I felt she had a story I wanted to learn more about.

One day a dark cloud came up and I mentioned that it was very black. All of the ladies said, "No, you shouldn't say that." Many Brazilians are superstitious about saying out loud anything that looks bad for fear that it will bring bad luck.

About that time, a loud clap of thunder jarred the room, and I happened to look at Darcy. Startled, she nearly jumped out of her seat as big tears begin to pour down her cheeks uncontrollably. Later I found out that the thunder had sounded like a loud gun shot which brought back memories of the death of her only daughter. Her daughter had shot herself and had died in her mother's arms when she was only 17 years old.

Darcy and her husband were devout Mormons until their daughter's death. They had been married in the Mormon Church where he was a deacon. In her heart she had started questioning their faith because of the Mormon teaching at that time that blacks could not be saved. (A few years later the Mormons changed that doctrine). It was enough, though, to make her want to examine other faiths. They had friends who were Spiritualists and others who were Jehovah Witnesses. Both she and her husband knew what the Catholics believed since they had been brought up as Catholics before being converted to Mormonism.

Soon after their daughter had committed suicide, their Spiritualist friends asked them to have a séance in their house so they could talk with their dead daughter and hear her say she was alright. (Oh, by-the-way, it is a predominate belief in Brazil that no person who commits suicide is going to heaven). Darcy had read enough Bible to know that to consult the dead was wrong, but her husband consented anyway. At the meeting they all joined hands in a circle and began their ceremony. Darcy bowed her head and said her own prayer, which went something like this, "Now, Lord, don't blame me with this; you know that I don't believe in it."

When she looked up, she was the only one standing. All of the others in the room had fallen down. That broke up that session.

She began to study the Jehovah Witnesses' doctrine and for a while was influenced by it. It was about that time that we met.

When Bro. Pires came to our church, I invited her to come hear him speak. She did and was greatly impressed by him because he reminded her so much of her father who had come from Portugal with his heavy accent typical of their country. (Just as the English speak a little differently from us, so do the Portuguese differ from the Brazilians in their speech.) In fact, she was so impressed that she went up to the front when he gave an invitation. She didn't have the foggiest idea of what she was doing, and I knew it. I asked her the next day if I could come visit her. After hearing more of God's Word, Darcy truly gave her heart to God at a later date. She is one of my many great sisters God gave me after I left my own to serve Him.

After their daughter's death, her husband turned against all forms of religion and remains an agnostic until this day, but he has a certain respect for us which we cherish.

We had an interesting experience one night about ten o'clock. A good friend of Darcy, who lived in Rio de Janeiro which was hundreds of miles away, called her in a very perturbed state of mind. This friend's son, who was crippled and was not able to walk very well, suddenly went wild. His mom carried him to the hospital and after the doctor gave him the strongest sedative possible, he still had unusual strength. He got up, threw furniture around, breaking tables and chairs. All the time he kept repeating, "Don't call Darcy." That puzzled his mother so she decided to call her to see if she knew why he didn't want Darcy to know. When they hung up the phone, Darcy jumped into her car and came to see us.

It was around ten o'clock at night, and for her to come at that hour, we knew something serious had happened. She wanted to know if the boy was demon possessed or not. People who are not up to date on what medicine can do to the human body may confuse wild behavior with demon possession. Just because a person is sick does not mean they have a demon. I can assure you that if medicine can cure the problem, that sickness is not demon possession. There are cases of real demon possession. Only God knows the difference. We should simply turn these cases over to Him instead of putting on a show and acting like we are so spiritual until by virtue of our power, God has to send these evil beings running. Parallel to the official religion of Brazil, Spiritualism (witchcraft, voodoo, necromancy, etc.) is practiced by many, so demon possession is fairly common.

Jeannie Montgomery

All we did was go into our house, kneel down, and ask God to handle this situation because we didn't even know what was wrong. Darcy went back home and the next morning her friend called to say that everything was alright. We still don't know if it were medicine or demons that brought all of this on, but either way, God took care of the problem and we are thankful.

After Darcy had been in our church awhile, she learned that there was a very elderly man who needed attention with a leg ulcer. Knowing that I had treated Arlindo's leg, she asked me to go with her to show her how to take care of him.

LAMPIÃO'S HUNTER

The frail old soldier lying on a cot in a single room house at the back of his daughter's land was the proud owner of an old wound inflicted by none other than the famous *Lampião* ("Oil Lamp"), a self styled Robin Hood of Brazil in the early 1900's. He and his band were criminals. It had been the soldier's duty to hunt down and bring in this very evasive fellow. Although he never caught him, he did receive a bullet souvenir that plagued him all of his life. Nothing short of an operation would cure this fellow. Anything that we could do would be superficial, but it was interesting to go and listen to his tales of bravado.

Pulling out a foot long knife from a night stand by his bed, he said he had to keep it handy to protect himself since he had "sent many people to hell with it." What was funny was one night Darcy managed to bring the old fellow to church and Steve preached on how we don't have to do anything to be condemned, but are condemned already if we did not believe in Jesus. It must have shaken him considerably, because after church, he told Darcy that Steve preached at him as if he were going to hell.

These My People

He never could get my name right. One time he would call me, "*Dona Menina* (Miss Girl)," the next, "*O Dona Efigênia*", which was the closest he could get to saying, Eugenia, but the funniest was when he called me "*Dona Oxigenia*" which means Miss Oxygen.

STEVEN AND REBEKAH LEAVE BRAZIL

My last two children decided to join their siblings in the States in May of 1980. Because Steven was Brazilian by birth, when he turned eighteen, he would have to serve the military and lose his U. S. citizenship. However, if he came to the States, he would not loose his Brazilian citizenship but maintain dual citizenship which we wanted. The decision for them to leave us and to come to the States was by far the hardest sacrifice we had ever faced. I felt that my arms and legs had been cut off and my heart ripped out. At the time, I didn't think that anyone cared about how we felt, but I was so wrong.

Fortunately, our work kept us very busy and we slowly adjusted to being reduced to only two once again.

THE END OF MILITARY DICTATORSHIP

From 1964 to 1984 we were never a part of what changed political history in Brazil, but we were eye witnesses of what happened during the entire twenty years of military rule. It was no secret that there was a big movement within the Catholic Church to accept communism all over Latin America. If my reader wonders why South America is so full of communistic leaders, here's the reason why, it was preached with fervor from their pulpits. As one country after another began to put in Communistic leaders, Brazilian's military became alarmed when a known communist, *Goulart*, was elected president of Brazil. There were stock piles of ammunition and propaganda hidden in parochial schools

Jeannie Montgomery

and seminaries. When the military decided to act, they did it swiftly and efficiently without bloodshed. They closed down temporarily church run institutions and took control of the government.

Goulart was slipped out of the country and General *Castelo Branco* took control. As for as our churches were concerned, the military didn't bother us at all. The only thing they did was send a police to a lot of our services which we were glad for them to do; the police and secret service men got to hear the gospel that way.

In 1984, twenty years later, the military was ready to turn over the government to the country in a democratic way. The first step was for Congress to elect a president for the whole country and during his term set up nationwide elections for the next. *Tancredo Neves*, a devoted lay preacher for the Catholic Church, was elected to do this job, but God had other plans.

Before *Neves* was elected, he went up a certain mountain to make promises to his saint at her shrine. (All of this was in the newspapers). The reporter, who got carried away with the emotion of it all and with his devotion to this saint, made an almost blasphemous statement: "Tancredo Neves is our Moses who went up into the mountain to pray and receive God's law for Brazil."

His statement made me fear. When men today get carried away with a fellow human being in such a way as to almost worship him, somebody had better look out. Trouble is on its way!

Neves was elected, but shortly before he could be sworn into office, he became ill with septicemia and nothing could cure him. There were vigils of varied denominations around the clock for a month all over the country to no avail. He died. Even the common people said that God did not want Neves in office for some reason.

These My People

We became apprehensive again about the political unrest in Brazil, but, thankfully, democracy, though fragile, took root and life continued in a normal way.

During all of our stay in Pereira Barreto, we worked simultaneously with the church at Sud Menucci.

CHAPTER ELEVEN
Special Problems In Sud Menucci
1977-1989

Our work continued to progress but with a lot of ups and downs. One problem we had to deal with was the loss of the church property in Sud Menucci. While we were in the States in 1984, another group came in and through some loophole of the law and with the help of one disgruntled member seized the property as their own. For five years our church met in homes and prayed for the return of our property. We finally got it back but not without paying a terrible price.

THE PRICE

Around noon one day Iracema, one of my oldest and dearest friends in Sud, called crying, "Jeannie, come. I need you." Then she proceeded to tell me that her oldest son was killed while he was out bush hogging. He had stirred up some killer bees, which caused them to swarm. He jumped off the tractor and fell under the bush hog's blade which sliced off the top of his head. She said that she wanted me to come because I knew what it was like to be without my children.

These My People

Outwardly, I was speechless, but inwardly I wanted to yell, "No, God! Not this one." Only the night before the boy had come to church, and sat through most of the service before his aunt got him to leave early to catch a bus. Like a lot of kids he had never given himself to the Lord but that night he had paid close attention and even sang with us. This boy that we knew from birth, who grew up with our kids, and became a young man, had suddenly left us without our knowing his destination. Words of comfort failed to come.

Steve and I got ready for what we knew would be an all night wake. Funerals in Brazil are not like the beautifully orchestrated burials in the U.S. where death in its rawest form is covered up. When we arrived, people had already begun to gather. Most wakes are in the homes as was this one. People spilled over into all the rooms and the yard. Some made coffee, but food is rarely ever brought in from the neighbors. I'll have to admit that the undertakers had done an excellent job on covering up the damaged part of the boy's head. Since the coffin was open from head to foot, they took wire mesh and cut out an oval opening big enough to cover most of his body including his hair line leaving only his face and chest areas open for viewing. In the mesh they put a layer of daisies that looked like a flower blanket covered him.

When we walked in, Iracema was quietly talking as she stood at the head of the coffin. She continued that way most of the night as she repeated, "Oh, it was awful. There was so much blood." While she talked, she cupped both hands and looked down as she slowly moved her fingers in the way she had scooped up his brains and had tenderly put them back into his skull. Her words painted such a vivid scene until the day I die, I will see the picture of a loving mother's hands dripping with blood as they held the remains of what was her son's vanished life.

Jeannie Montgomery

The Lord has a purpose for things that happen in a Christian's life. All of our church gathered in the yard to have funeral services along with a huge number of friends. One person from the group who had taken our church property from us also came. After the services he came up to Steve at the graveside and asked, "Who were all those people who sang hymns and prayed?"

"They are our church members," Steve replied.

"Are you telling me that these are the members of the original church which we were told had died?"

"Yes."

The guy was so shocked that his church had been deceived until he purposed in his heart to set things right. Although it took a few months to do that, we did get our property back. To our surprise when we all returned to the building, it was too small for our congregation! Immediately, plans were made to build a larger building, and call a Brazilian pastor. The church saw both of these goals reached soon, by the grace of God.

After Bro. Helmut arrived we were again free to travel. He was the one to lead the church in rebuilding.

But before we left, disaster struck again.

MARIO AND MARIA

If you remember, Mario and Maria were some of the original members of the Pioneiros Church. When we met them, they had four children, a girl and three boys. Maria had birthed other children; but because of being far from hospital care, she lost at least two at birth in very traumatic ways, but the four grew up to become responsible adults. The daughter married and moved to a town near Sao Paulo. The oldest son did very well and became a bank manager for an important

These My People

bank in Sao Paulo. The two younger sons remained in Sud Menucci with their parents. (They are presently lay preachers in the Sud Church even as I write).

Maria's niece, *Dirce*, who worked at the local hospital, informed me at church that Maria had cancer but didn't know it yet. She was to go to the doctor the next day to receive the results. Then Maria herself told me that she was going in for the results the next day. That gave me the chance to ask her, "Would you like for me to go with you?" She looked at me with the sweetest look and a broad smile on her face as she said, "No, Sister, I'm alright. I'm not afraid of dying." So that meant her body had already told her what she had and she was ready to go.

The following week her banker son came out to Sud to get his mother to take her to Sao Paulo where she could get better treatment. They traveled at night and about 3:00 a.m. stopped at his sister's house to rest a bit. During the stay, his sister asked him about his soul. His reply was, "If I die tonight, I'm going straight to hell." The sad thing is that within an hour it happened. When they got back into the car to finish the rest of the trip, a dense fog settled in as they neared Sao Paulo and he could not see the pillars that held up an overpass. The crash threw some of them out of the car but he was killed instantly. Maria lived a few hours and died.

In Pereira Barreto we learned of the wreck from the police. We immediately got our things ready to travel and went to Sud to see if we could find Mario's teenage sons who had stayed behind. At this point none of us knew who all had been killed but were told they were all in the hospital. The boys were out in the village, trying to find someone to take them to see their parents. We gathered them up and headed to the hospital. It took us about eight hours to get there and Maria died just before we arrived. Mario was injured and in shock. He was talking nonstop. His son's pregnant wife was also hurt but survived.

Her people who were Spiritualists had already come to the hospital and were trying to calm Mario down. After we had tried to talk with Mario, we decided to pray. As Steve began to pray, Mario immediately calmed down and was quiet. During the prayer one of the people in the room started crying out loud, "He died, he died." I guess she thought that our praying had sent him on to glory. While Steve finished the prayer, I had to calm the poor distraught soul.

Since burial has to be within twenty-four hours, the in-laws decided to bury both Maria and son in Sao Paulo the next day. To my surprise they were buried in what is considered the cemetery of the elite. I didn't realize until then how high up in society the son had gone. There were important people there. It was one of the hardest funerals Steve had ever preached. On one side lay one of the sweetest women that ever breathed, and on the other lay a son she would never see again. Steve preached about the faith and hope that Maria had and concluded by saying that we will leave the fate of the son in God's hands.

Back in Pereira we made our final plans to travel to the States. Bro. Helmut and wife moved out from São Paulo to take our place. The weekend before we left, we went out to Sud to tell everyone goodbye. When services were over and nearly everyone had left, Iracema came to tell me goodbye. Her words were, "Jeannie, go with God and see your children." Crying she dropped her head on my shoulder as mine dropped on hers. Our cry was the cry of "Rachel weeping for her children, and would not be comforted, because they are not."

We came back for a short visit to the States and then returned to Pereira Barretto to work until we were asked to go to Ourinhos to help start a new church there.

CHAPTER TWELVE
OURINHOS
1989-2001

WHEN WE LEFT THE PEREIRA Barreto-Sud Menucci area for a trip back to the States, we had been on the mission field for 36 years. Without a clue as to where the Lord would have us to work next, we gave ourselves over to prayer, asking for God's guidance. When the answer to our prayers came, we didn't have a doubt about our "Macedonian call." Two families in the city of Ourinhos sent us letters asking us to come and start a church in their town. For several years we had considered working in that area, so this sealed our decision to move there.

Ourinhos, with its population of about seventy thousand, is one of those small interior towns where Italians settled at the turn of the twentieth century. Located on the Tropic of Capricorn and only a few miles within the border of the State of Sao Paulo with its southern neighbor, the State of Paraná, it is surrounded by endless miles of sugar cane fields. It is common to see the fields burning somewhere around the city as that particular section is being prepared for the harvest. Nearly all of the cane is used to make alcohol fuel for cars. In other words we had moved to the "green oil" fields of Brazil. When it comes to developing alternative fuels, Brazil is far ahead of other countries. We had landed right in the middle of its renewable energy source, sugar cane.

Since Brazil became a nation, economy determines its social lines, that is, rich versus poor, rather than race. There was virtually no middle class, but Ourinhos did not fit the norm. From the start our congregation was frequented by teachers, principals, lawyers, and occasionally doctors. The overall better standard of living of the common people showed in their houses; even our house was better than what we had before. For the first in Brazil, we had running hot water in the bathrooms although the former owner didn't bother to put it in the kitchen.

MY BRAZILIAN DEBORAH

Before we moved to Ourinhos there was a member of the church in Sud Menucci who had a child born almost completely deaf. At that time she wanted to give the little girl, Deborah, to me because she knew she could never teach her what she needed to know. I thought it would be very cruel to remove a child, who didn't even know her full name, from home which was the only secure place she had ever known. Now that Deborah was sixteen, I decided to take her to see if I could get her in a special school in Ourinhos and also work with her myself. To keep her family ties intact we took her back to her home periodically.

During the preceding ten years with all my children gone, I had gradually given myself over to growing old. At fifty-seven I had to bounce back to life and sharpen up my intellect considerably. Every passing hour of the day with Deborah was a walking classroom. She brought young life into my heart again and I hoped and prayed that somehow I could plant a little knowledge of eternal life into hers.

These My People

Soon after she came to live with us, I had to go grocery shopping on the other side of town. Steve stayed home to rest, and I took Deborah with me. The day was very foggy. Returning home I didn't see the speed bump until I hit it hard enough to make us both bounce to the roof of the car. Fortunately, neither was hurt. That thrilled Deborah so much she could hardly wait to tell Steve. Although she didn't know one word in Portuguese or in sign language, she ran into the house and very graphically showed Steve what I had done. With her around there would be no secrets in our house!

Every time we went somewhere by foot, I worried about her getting run over by a car until the day she saved me from stepping out in front of an oncoming vehicle. When that happened, we had already learned enough sign language to communicate with each other so I asked her how she knew the car was coming. "I could feel the vibrations," she replied. My worrying stopped right there. I learned that God compensates people with deficiencies with extra sensibilities that normal people don't have.

When her seventeenth birthday rolled around, she wanted to know how old she was. I decided to give her a party. Instead of a big cake I made cup cakes and put candles on seventeen of them. Anything and everything became a teaching tool.

She stayed with me a year and an half, but the nearest I got to making her understand the gospel was shortly before she left. We had the Lord's Supper at church and afterwards I brought the left over elements to the house. As I was cleaning the cups, she watched me intently. I explained to her how Jesus had died for us and had shed his blood to cover our sins and how the Lord's Supper was to commemorate that. When I finished, tears welled up in her eyes as she shook her head and said, "I didn't know." I pray that someone may yet teach her more truth. She returned to her home and later I heard that she had married a deaf boy.

ZILDA

We lived only an half of a block away from one of the families who wrote us about coming to work in Ourinhos. Zilda was the superintendent of schools in our area. Her husband Toribio was a businessman until he was incapacitated by a serious infection which required a kidney transplant. Zilda was a believer who was tormented by the teachings of her church that she could lose her salvation. One day she read a book by the ex-priest, Anibal Reis, on the eternal security of the believer. The scriptures he presented calmed her fears but made her want to be a part of a secure people. She met a member of our church from Santa Cruz and was thrilled to find a people who believed as the ex-priest did. All of this happened before we moved to Ourinhos. A person might say that because of these contacts the Ourinhos Church was born.

Zilda was a remarkable lady. She was in and out of the governor's palace at least once a month and knew all the important people around while at the same time she was as unsophisticated and humble a person as one could meet.

Because Zilda's faith was evident in her life, people respected her at work, and she often was called upon to help resolve difficult situations. For example, one day a disturbed woman came to her with a problem no one wants or knows how to deal with. The lady had a teenage sister who had contracted HIV from her promiscuous life style. The girl gave birth to an infected baby. Angry with God and the whole world, she dashed the baby against the wall killing it. She was not put in jail because she was a minor. Knowing that she would probably die from the disease, she went out into the streets and slept with as many men as she could so they would also become infected. But, that wasn't enough; she wanted her family to have the disease also. In a fit of rage, she took a syringe and needle, drew her own blood, and went around trying to squirt it on her sister's children. The lady herself was ready to commit suicide. She went to Zilda looking for help. Zilda took her home and worked with her and the teenager until things calmed down.

Above all, Zilda loved to teach the Bible and did so in as many homes as she could. She was instrumental in bringing many women to church.

She was always a faithful friend to me as well as being a good neighbor. Her husband was such a nervous busy type person until one day I told him that when he died, he would walk a block before he dropped. He was very helpful in building our church house, doing most of the work himself.

A TEACHER

Among the teachers Zilda brought to church was a lady who had serious marital problems. Her husband ran around and lived with another woman, but wanted his wife to sit complacently at home. He didn't like it one bit when she decided to come to our church. Once he convinced her to go with him to a farm to see a horse he said he was buying for their son. Instead, he took her to a place the locals called "The Assassin's Rock." There he demanded that she tell him who was the man she was going to meet when she went to our church. At first, she thought about just saying there wasn't anyone, but she knew he would not believe her. Her answer to him was wonderful. "Yes, I went there to meet a man and his name is Jesus". That did not satisfy him because he wanted to kill her. As he was coming down with the

Jeannie Montgomery

knife, her arm automatically flew up to protect herself. The knife sliced into her arm but did not hit any vital organ. When he saw the blood start pouring out of her arm, he went berserk, and rushed her to the hospital. All of this trouble did not keep her from coming to church. She came until she moved away. (Incidentally, the man did not go to jail for this.)

Once a lady in Texas asked me if I had television in Brazil. When I answered in the affirmative, she said, "I'm so glad, because you won't get bored if you have one." Inside myself I smiled at the thought of being bored with so much going on. We had the real thing, not some imaginary story. Homesick for family, yes? Bored, never! We barely got out of one situation before we were in the big middle of another, for example, like Steve making a quick trip to Africa.

A QUICK TRIP TO MALAWI

In February of 1992 a church in California asked Steve to go with their pastor to Malawi on a fact finding tour to check out the possibilities of starting a mission among several native groups who had requested help. I stayed in the States while Steve went on this trip.

By the time Steve reached New York, I was having a major medical crisis in Louisiana. A tenacious little fellow in Brazil had latched onto the retina of my left eye and had ruined a third of my vision. The parasite had caused my eye to bleed, temporarily blinding me on that side. At first, the doctor thought I would have to fly to Houston for very special treatment, but with further examination he decided to treat it locally.

In the meantime, the mission group had a good trip over, but once there, every move they made was observed suspiciously by the police. They were informed that they couldn't hold a public service or baptize.

Resorting to holding meetings under trees or in homes, they were able to lay the ground work for the next trip which was two years later. They stayed two weeks working from sunup till late at night under very harsh conditions. When the group returned to the States, the church had a large number of contacts with whom they corresponded regularly.

Steve came to Louisiana where I recuperated my vision. Although one third of it had been lost, the good eye compensated for it and my 20/20 vision came back. God is so good to me!

We returned to Brazil and resumed our work in Ourinhos, but in 1994 Steve went again with the group. Somehow I always seemed to come down with a serious problem when Steve was gone.

MY COUSIN BO, A NURSE SENT BY GOD

I was sitting at home so peaceful I felt like going to sleep, never to wake up which was exactly what was about to happen if God had not sent me a special person, in fact, a registered nurse. About the time I was giving in to the urge to sleep, a distant cousin I barely knew came with a letter for me to translate. She had never been to my house before. As I began to talk and to translate, I slowly began to get weaker and weaker. When I could barely talk, she saw something was wrong and called my sister who took me to the emergency room at a local hospital; from there I went straight to the ICU. Thanks to the Good Lord I was out of there in a couple of days and went back home.

What can I say? Bo saved my life. I never saw her again; she died before we came back to the States. My heart will always cry out a big, "Thank you, Bo"!

During all the above Steve and the group with him were having good success in Africa. They were able to organize several churches and get a lot of teaching done. Though feeble in its beginnings, the work there has carried on. The spiritual and physical needs were and still are tremendous.

THE LAST TRACT

On the last day of their stay in Malawi they stopped to fill up the rental car with gas before returning it. While the others were doing that, Steve began to hand out more of the gospel tracts he had in the Chichewa language. People began to form a line to receive a tract and Steve passed them out very quickly. As he was finishing up, one man's request moved his heart deeply. He said, "Mister, do you have a word from God for me today?"

A true missionary always wants to give this word from the Lord Jesus Christ to the needy soul: "Come unto me, all ye that labour and are heavy laden and I will give you rest." Matthew 11:28.

On Steve's return trip he brought home with him a reminder that he had been to Africa, malaria. By the time he arrived in Louisiana he was almost delirious. Again God saw fit to arrange things for us. Probably the only doctor in Alexandria who had ever treated malaria "just happened" to be working in the ER that day. He suspected that Steve had a dreaded type of malaria found in Africa. For this type of malaria there is a one dose treatment which drug stores don't bother to carry here because the disease is no longer found in the U.S. Guess what? Someone had gone to Africa the year before and had come home with the same disease. There was one dose of his medicine left over, waiting for Steve to use it a year later. That along with heavy doses of quinine put in check the little parasite in Steve's body. With our health fairly under control, we were soon able to travel again to Brazil.

Back in Brazil our world traveler son, David, moved in with us to settle down. He had worked around the globe and wanted to come back to Brazil to live. Wherever David is, things liven up for he is a roomful all by himself. He briefly moved his office into my living room until he was able to rent a house nearby. For some time, I had his secretary, Flavio, in my house in business hours. Soon I had his secretary's girl friend, *Brigitte* (*Brí* for short), move in to stay with us while she went to college. My house bustled once more with people coming and going.

FLAVIO AND JANDER

When David's office was in my living room, I not only had him back home but also had Flavio most of the time during the week. Also his brother, Jander would drop in quite frequently. These two fine young men have been faithful in God's service since the beginning of our church in Ourinhos. They are especially helpful to their present pastor.

About that time a very musically talented young member decided to train a choir for our church.

BRUNO AND THE SINGERS

Bruno, Zilda's nephew, was born with a true Italian ear for music. If he heard a tune, he could sit down immediately at the piano and pick out the tune with one finger. He had "an ear for music" so we encouraged his parents to send him to music school. By the time he was sixteen he was playing classical music for the city's orchestra.

He started training the church group to sing a cappella. None of them knew one note from another, nor how to sing the scale. But with Flavio and Jander, who had never sung anything in their lives, he really hit a snag, big time! About when he was ready to give up on ever teaching them to sing, I asked David for him to let me have

Jeannie Montgomery

Flavio for thirty minutes every morning when he came to work. I am not a music teacher but I knew that if he were to ever carry a tune he would have to have it drilled into his head. He could have easily passed as an absolute monotone. After a month he went back to the choir and surprised everyone. He could carry a tune! Bruno asked me how I managed to make such a difference in Flavio. First let me say, that God had a plan in store for Flavio and next, he just needed someone to hold his feet to the fire while he learned. I began by making him learn to play Thompson's Beginner's lessons and as he hit each note, he had to sing it. I laughed to myself when he argued with me that Brazilians learn to memorize music and that reading wasn't necessary. Stubbornly, I simply stated, "But you are going to learn to read." As time passed he not only learned to read and sing but became the church's main pianist when Bruno is not around. He also knows how to direct the choir. He has Bruno to thank for the discipline of a cappella singing.

Bruno worked with another member of the church who had a natural bent for music, Israel.

ISRAEL

Israel was a sweet easy going young fellow who was a comfortable person to be around. Steve began having one of the young men take a turn at giving a Bible lesson once a month to the whole church. Shortly, we had a group of them who could not only sing but could speak as well as many preachers can preach.

When we left Ourinhos, the church called a pastor who didn't stay long so they had to call another. Sometime prior to that, Israel let it be known that the Lord was dealing with him about preaching. He didn't know where God wanted him to work but was willing to go wherever the Lord would lead him. When the church found itself without a pastor, they called him. He accepted and is there today, leading the church and its two preaching points in other cities nearby.

But before we left Ourinhos other things happened as well. One night as we were ending our services, a disturbed woman slipped in and sat on the back bench. She told me that she had come to look for peace.

BETTE

Bette's story is the same as that of untold hundreds of abused wives. Her husband at one time held a good job, but he in his prosperity began to hang out with the wrong crowd, became a drunkard, and a dope addict which cost him his job. Because of his aggressiveness, she and her two children could not live with him. Many times going to and from her house she passed our church, and when she heard our singing, she knew God was with us. There seemed to be something drawing her into where we were, but at the same time she was afraid to do so. Finally, she got so desperate, she ran into our building even though it was when we were singing the last song. Later she grew stronger and began to learn the way of salvation. The night she was baptized, the house was full. As we were all going by to welcome her into our church, her husband came in the door near where we all were. Irate and vulgar, he said all manner of bad things. Knowing we had a volatile situation on hand, Steve caught him by the arm and walked him outside. As Steve talked to him, he positioned the guy in such a way as to have his back to us ladies. All of the ladies gathered around Bette, putting her in the middle, and we walked as a unit by the man without him seeing his wife. Zilda took her home while we stayed behind with Bette's husband. When he finally left in the opposite direction than to his house, we thought all was well and went home.

Jeannie Montgomery

It is unbelievable what happened next. Bette went home and locked up but her husband came and tried to break in anyway. He was shouting, "I'm going to kill you. I'm going to kill you." In her newly found peace she prayed, "Lord, I don't want to die. I want to live and raise my children but my life's in your hands." When she finished praying, she went to the kitchen, picked up a butcher knife, and went outside to him. She extended her hand with the knife and said, "Here, take it and kill me". His hands flew up in fear as if he had seen a ghost. Screaming and hurriedly backing away from her he backed to the far side of the road and fell off, tumbling down a steep decline onto a busy highway where he lay unconscious until the police found him. Her fear of him was gone! Nevertheless, he did not leave her alone. On another occasion he tried to scare her by jumping over the back wall of the church so he could come in without anyone seeing him; but God saw him. The fence is high and he misjudged the distance as he jumped. When he landed on his feet, both of them broke. (Some people have a hard time learning that you don't tangle with God. He wins every time!)

There was a young boy living near Bette who sympathized with her. He had been abused as a young child, so for obvious reasons I will not give his real name but simply call him Sonny.

SONNY

The first time I saw him was at church one Sunday morning when he came with Bette. He listened attentively. As they were walking out, Bette paused to tell me again how she had found peace. Sonny tried to say what he felt but didn't have the vocabulary to do so. He just looked up and said, "I feel like this." Then he rubbed his heart and breathed out a sigh of relief. Immediately, he won my heart. When I heard his story, I was determined to spend as much time with him as I could. At the age of four he was sexually abused by a man. When his father heard about it, he blamed Sonny's mother, and left her to raise him alone. Sonny and his mother moved in with his grandmother, leaving him without a father figure. When he became of school age, he was almost impossible to control in the classroom. Other kids agitated him by calling him a gay and said all manner of bad things about him.

Without any idea if he had talent or not, I asked him to come to my house for music lessons three times a week for the purpose of getting to know him. It didn't take long to see he had exceptional talent waiting to be tapped.

After several months of studying, he wanted to play a hymn at church. His big desire was to "flower up" a hymn. He had already learned the basic three note position of a root cord. Since this was his first time to play for congregational singing, I told him not to dare try "to flower up" the song on his first attempt to accompany our singing. He needed only to read and play the written notes. He proudly went to the piano and played without a flaw until he got to the end. Suddenly the urge to flower up the end of the song was just too great! He took his right hand and started at the bass end and banged out the root cord with intentions of going from one end of the piano to the other with one hand. When his hand got to the middle of the piano, the time ran out on the hymn, but he was determined to finish his run anyway. With no one singing he finished his run as he looked over at me and grinned. By that time we all were laughing. When I got him to myself, I gave him a scolding. "Don't ever try to flower up a song unless you do it within the proper time beat."

Sheepishly he laughed, "That's right. I had more flowers than I had vases to put them in."

After we had moved to the States and were visiting Brazil two years ago, I was amazed at how well the flowers tumbled out of his fingers into the vase with perfect timing as his fingers ran up and down the keyboard. Sonny Boy was now a young adult and could play very well! I just hope and pray that his talent will be used in the Lord's work. He and Bette both will have to really fight if they keep on the right path because the odds are against them, although all things are possible with God.

After having taught young people music, two deaf girls, numerous people English as a second language, and my own children, I have often wondered why the Lord didn't lay it on my heart to be a teacher before I married. It seemed that was what I had to do whether I knew what I was doing or not. With every lesson my heart cried to God to make them understand because I was deficient and not educated. My next experience with teaching was monumental in what God can do when there is a heart yearning to know the Word of the Lord.

ANESIA OF OURINHOS

One day when some of the church men were out passing out tracts, they gave one to a sixty-six year old lady who gladly received it. She came to the very next service. God opened her understanding how to be saved and she turned to Him. The day she was baptized, her husband became so infuriated, his blood pressure shot up. Just as we were getting ready to baptize *Anésia,* her daughter came buzzing up to take her to the hospital where her husband was seeing a doctor. Instead of getting perturbed she simply said, "I am going to be baptized. Then I will go." She was determined to follow the Lord.

About a week later, she asked me if I could come visit her to read the Bible to her. She longed for the Word of God, but could not read.

She was from that era when many did not learn to read. I had heard that her husband was an angry man, and, frankly, I was a little concerned about what would happen when I went. The first day, I didn't even see him, but the next time I went, he walked by and gave me a stern look without bothering us.

Our reading progressed and the thought crossed my mind that a newborn Christian needs to know how to pray. That took us to Matthew 6 for our reading. I didn't try to explain anything; I just read. The next time I went she told me that she had smoked since she was a child and could not get the day started without her cup of coffee and cigarette. In fact, her whole family smoked but now that she was a Christian, she felt that she should stop. To break her lifetime habit she knew that God had to help her if she succeeded. After our reading about fasting she decided to drink no more coffee until she had broken the habit since a cup of coffee had to have the accompanying cigarette. God heard her prayer and delivered her from her nicotine bondage the very first week of her conversion without any of us telling her she had to give up this or that to be an effective Christian. The Holy Spirit taught her heart what to do.

I soon realized that she needed to read the Bible for herself. She consented and we purchased first grade readers. It seemed ridiculous that the blind would lead the blind in learning to read. Of course, I could read and speak Portuguese but not nearly well enough to teach a native the true phonetic sounds. But since when did not being equipped, stop a person from making an effort? God blessed beyond measure. Anesia began reading within a month. An amazing thing happened; when her husband saw that she could read, he asked her to read to him. He had gone to every spiritualistic and charismatic healer he could find to heal him of his incurable emphysema. When they couldn't do anything for him, he became bitter and angry against religion. Even so, back in the recesses of his heart he longed for God because he knew he was going to die soon. When they were alone, she was able to do what he wouldn't let anyone else do and that was to give him the Word of God. I had only given her basic phonics, but God had taught her to read in a hurry so her husband could hear words of life. The night before he died, he called for Steve to come to the hospital so he could hear more. Anesia thought that he made peace with his maker before he died. At his funeral Steve was able to speak to a large number of his rough incredulous friends about how he had heard the Word.

After he died, Anesia settled the family's property and moved near a daughter in another town. She carried with her the priceless treasure of the Word of God.

We, too, had some changes. A church in Sao Paulo needed help so we started going back and forth between Ourinhos and Sao Paulo every month. We had to face many heart breaking problems which were not of our making nor were we desirous to deal with them, but to save the church we did. God blessed in so many sweet ways. Almost daily we saw His Hand working.

On one of our trips we were invited to a church where we had never been. If "feeling led" were the criteria for knowing God's leading, then something was badly wrong with me. I didn't even want to go. As soon as we arrived at church, the pastor came up to us and simply said, "Bro. Steve, I want you to take the men and teach them during this service and I want Sis. Eugenia to take the women." Immediately, I said, no, that it would be better for Steve to do the teaching. The pastor would not change his mind. Within a few minutes I found myself in a roomful of women and girls of all ages. My mind was as blank as a white sheet of paper. I was introduced and called up front. Looking out on the group I thought, "What in the world am I going to say?" Since I didn't have some spiritual Bible lesson ready, I simply started talking to the little girls about moral conduct and then went on up by age group. When I got to the young married women, interest became tense. Suddenly, a young lady spoke up and said, "My husband and I are separated. He said he didn't love me anymore. Now he wants me back, but he hurt my feelings."

"Did he apologize?" I asked.

"Yes, Ma'am."

"Did he say he loved you?"

"Yes, Ma'am".

"Do you love him"?

"Yes, Ma'am".

"What are you waiting for? You get on that phone right now and call him."

At that point I didn't know what to expect. Everyone in the room turned to her, not to me, and clapped. She was the pastor's daughter. I was beginning to see why I was there. Our meeting lasted two hours with questions and answers. As the women filed by me to say goodbye, a young girl whispered, "Could I talk to you alone"?

We went into a small room where she told me her plight. She could not forgive her father who had molested her.

I took her in my arms as we both cried. My answer to her was, *"Run, little girl, run; this sin is not yours."*

God surely spoke through Balaam's stubborn donkey that Sunday when he used me. No matter what I might have felt about going, I learned that I have a lot of people out there in the world that I haven't met yet. When we do meet, there will be an instant bonding. God's people are that way.

Our work in Sao Paulo and in Ourinhos ended at the same time. Both places called native pastors; simultaneously we received a call to come back to Corinth to work. All of a sudden it seemed that our lives had made full circle and we found ourselves right where we had started off to the foreign fields forty-seven years before.

Before we left Brazil, we had the heart wrenching task of going around to all the churches to tell them goodbye. As I looked over the crowds, I saw hundreds of faces, each with a story worth telling. To borrow Sonny's words about his music, "I have more flowers than I have vases to put them in." I cannot put all my people between two book covers.

When John's heavenly vision turns to reality and I shall see people with whom I have worked, worshiping the Lamb among that great number, then let me shout, "Thank you, Father, for all of *these my people.*"

I sincerely hope you will be one of them, too.

About the Author

Eugenia Montgomery, native of rural Central Louisiana, entered active foreign mission work when she married her missionary husband. They have been married fifty-four years, forty-seven of which were spent in Japan and Brazil.

At her table foreign languages and foods are as common as the English language and potatoes. She has faced difficult situations from which only God could have delivered. Her goal in life is to honor Him.

As the mother of six children, grandmother of fifteen, and counselor to an untold number of troubled people, she knows that life is stranger than fiction and that all human beings are basically the same around the world, even here in Central Louisiana.

Made in the USA
Columbia, SC
25 January 2025